27

A Birdwatcher's Cookbook

ALSO BY ERMA J. FISK

The Peacocks of Baboquivari

Parrots' Wood

The Bird with the Silver Bracelet

ERMA J. FISK

A Birdwatcher's Cookbook

Illustrations by Louise Russell

W · W · NORTON & COMPANY · NEW YORK · LONDON

The text of this book is composed in Garamond, with display type set in Cochin
Italic.
Composition and manufacturing by The Maple-Vail Book Manufacturing Group.

First Edition

Library of Congress Cataloging-in-Publication Data

Fisk, Erma J.
  A birdwatcher's cookbook / Erma J. Fisk.
    p.   cm.
  Includes index.
  1. Cookery.   I. Title.
TX715.F543   1987
641.5—dc19   87-18748
                                    CIP

ISBN 0-393-02502-0

W. W. Norton & Company, Inc., 500 Fifth Avenue, New York, N.Y. 10110
W. W. Norton & Company Ltd., 37 Great Russell Street, London WC1B 3NU

1 2 3 4 5 6 7 8 9 0

To the many friends who encouraged this project and contributed to it, but especially to Lisa Russell.

Contents

CONTENTS

Warning

Statement 1

This cookbook is not for those who stop at a deli or neighborhood fruit stand to pick up what is needed for the evening meal. It presupposes a woman, or man, to whom cooking is pleasure and hobby as well as necessity, or one who must keep a tight hand on expenses and so be willing to invest in time rather than in the alluringly boxed, expensive packages on market shelves. It isn't for single parents who collect children on their way home from work, face laundry and house cleaning and loneliness when they unlock their doors. These people must expend their creative energies in other ways. We each have to work out our own life style. Or do we? Is it the hand of fate, as some believe, or accident that sets us on roads we didn't envisage? Do we really decide our goals as we wash the dishes, put our children to bed? I often wonder.

Statement 2

I am not a methodical cook. I was pitchforked into my first kitchen when the ink of my Vassar College diploma was still wet. A competence in French literature and field hockey was not useful. Our family cook used to chase us four children out of her way with a broom so she wouldn't step on us as she stirred, so I learned to cook by guess and by gosh. The first time I baked a potato, the *Fanny Farmer* I'd been given (and wish I still had) said only to bake a potato until it was tender. Timorously I had inquired of the woman across our apartment hall as to whether this might mean 20 minutes or 2 hours—a reasonable query, I still feel. She never let me forget.

Statement 3

I know—and respect—men cooks. But since the large percentage of my acquaintances are women, I will hereafter refer to cooks as *she*. What this modern, bisexual world needs is a bisexual pronoun.

Statement 4

Whether for man or woman, the recipes here presented (except perhaps the last two) presuppose a kitchen whose shelves and

refrigerator hold the standard necessities—flour, sugar, seasonings, herbs, milk, eggs (the only egg I once found in a
male cook's fridge was three weeks old—maybe five, he told
me cheerfully. What did I want an egg for?), oil and vinegar,
rolled oats, shortening, corn meal, molasses, chocolate, nuts,
raisins, coconut, legumes (that's peas and beans). You will find
more as you read these pages. You can't go running to the
store every time you start a meal, not if you live miles distant.
I have good friends who live *sixty* miles from market. They eat
like kings, are always feeding friends. They have a big back
pantry, though, and are more organized than I am. Quantity
will depend upon how many you are planning to feed. Two,
four, eight, eighteen? Most recipes claim to be for four or six,
but this depends upon appetites. My friends are outdoor types,
birdwatchers, young men and women. They like sweets and
lots of everything. You can put leftovers, if any, into soup or
out on your bird feeder. So double or triple or more my
instructions, but *you* have to make such decisions—I can only
spoon-feed you so far.

Statement 5

This book is for creative cooks, those who don't hesitate to
toss yesterday's leftovers into this morning's scrambled eggs or
into luncheon soup, as I said; who substitute when they lack
an ingredient; who change recipes on whim. It's for people
who cook for fun or out of desperation. If guests are hungry,
they will eat anything, I've found, especially if they are sitting
about the kitchen or standing (usually in the way) while you
bustle about, tantalizing them with fragrances from your kettles. I've tested most of these dishes. Some I don't particularly

like but others do, so maybe you will. I present relatively accurate measurements but don't always stick to them. I find cooking by rote boring. On the other hand, some of the finest cooks I know never deviate from their instructions by one pinch or splash. I don't know how they manage this. If one egg enriches a dish, why aren't two better? If your file card calls for acorn squash, what is wrong with using butternut or pumpkin?

It's the difference between dancing—with freedom to improvise, to kiss your partner midstep—and jogging. However *you* do it, good luck.

Be sure to use really good cheeses.

Statement 6

I *know* that cooking takes time. So does knitting, tending a garden, writing poetry, driving children to the dentist, volunteering at a hospital. I had to decide once whether to keep on working at a menial office job that bored me horribly but paid for a cleaning woman and other luxuries or to work at home, where I was available to our children and their friends, to my own friends; where my husband would find me when he came wearily in from work; where, to a reasonable degree, I could set my own hours and obligations.

Years later, a friend of one of our sons showed up unheralded, nervously needing dinner and a bed for the night. He stood in the hallway while our dog and I sniffed him. He himself was sniffing a smell from the kitchen. He sighed and set down his backpack, his hesitancy evaporated.

"Irving told me it would smell like this here," he said. "Cinnamon buns?"

Warning

You never know what you are building in this world; you never know how the payment will come back to you.

Statement 7

I know excellent men cooks, good at grilling steak and chicken, at fish and potatoes, at eggnog. Many have gourmet skills. But the majority of my male friends are not about to leave their bird chasing to prepare a dinner. Only dark and weariness and thirst bring them in. They spend the night before any jaunt not cooking, but checking maps, gathering equipment, filling thermoses, talking on the telephone. If they are single, come home alone or with a companion, they "pull something out of the freezer," they tell me.

"But what do you do when there are half a dozen of you," I persisted, "and you want to sit around convivially checking lists, deciphering your notes, talking?"

They looked at me in astonishment. "Go to a restaurant, of course," they answered. "Or take Tom (or Dick or Harry) with us—his wife is always good for a dinner."

Maybe Tom, Dick, and Harry have this obligation written in their marriage contracts. I don't know. A woman who marries a birder has to be aware of the rules.

Introduction

I came late to the sport and studies of birdwatching, so I embraced these with passion—at first racing off on day or weekend excursions, later, as I learned more, on trips to Central America, to the Caribbean islands, and to South America. This was in the days before organized tours, before birders and photographers lurked behind every bush, in every hotel lobby, picking each others' brains on "Where to Go Next for What." Our living, and especially our eating, was often primitive. The adventure went out of this when tourism tramped in on our heels, beds and potable water, boat engines and transportation becoming reliable—well, fairly reliable. By then I had become tired of looking at the hind ends of birds I really couldn't see all that well up there in forest leaves, out there on a pitching sea. So I put what knowledge I had acquired into birdbanding. I worked the fall migrations—first in the Northeast, later in south Florida. I took my tools and accompanied researchers to Mexico, to tropical islands, to Ecuador and Arizona, honing my identification skills on birds in the hand instead of the bush. In those early days, migrant birdbanders were rarities, not today's annual crop of eager young biologists wanting field rather than office work. You didn't find in swamps and pas-

tures, on beaches and in forest remnants, the businessmen and
-women who now pour out of their offices on weekends, chasing, listing, studying birds with binoculars and telescopes and
cameras, needing hearty breakfasts to sustain them, appreci-
ating something besides peanut butter and jelly for lunch,
gathering happily at dusk to eat dinner and argue their finds.

It was a joyous life. I slept in palaces of splendor long past,
in inns of varied comforts, in motels, in hovels. Only once in
a tent—surprisingly. There might be eight of us scattered about
on couches or the floor, strangers in a double bed. Eagerness,
not sex, ruled our lives. And for me, always, there was a kitchen.

Banders, and the birdwatchers who come to watch banders,
eat. Even the most avid listers. Sometimes at midnight; sometimes, if they are netting shore birds or hunting owls, at 4:30
A.M. Nutritional demands are constant. With my domestic
background, I seemed always to end up in kitchens. It might
be watching in horror as a surly Ecuadorian cook pounded
parrot breasts and hard green plantains to leather, then fried
these to tooth-defying texture. It might be standing on a peb-
bly Canadian beach watching a guide bake bannock (that's
simple biscuit mix carried in a sack and moistened with lake
water) in a heavy skillet that was tilted over coals, while the
fish we had caught sizzled beside it and a loon—or a wolf—
called in the distance. At one Mexican "inn," my only access
to the tiny kitchen, once I had shoved my way through a herd
of cows, was a small window, where I and my limping Spanish
became fixtures, observing a plump señora and her two daugh-
ters skillfully skirt each other while, with quick flicks of their
wrists, they added the seasonings and oils and strange vegetables that increased the flavor of our simple foods and of an
endless stream of small tortillas they cooked to our order while
rain beat down and wind blew through the canvas that pro-

tected our dining trestle, if not our backs. In Arizona, I learned to keep a sturdy soup on my tiny mesquite-heated stove for climbers in need of comfort who might come limping from the mountain that reared its bulk above me.

The staple fare of birders lacks variety and seems everywhere to be much the same: doughnuts (of the country—these can be adventuresome); peanut butter and grape jelly; a rectangle of cheese. These still the clamor of a stomach but don't do much else for you. Once on a grocery run to a Mexican village, I begged our leader: Please, couldn't he buy a jar of marmalade to go with our peanut butter? His eyes frosted. It would be five cents more from a tight budget, he admonished me, reaching for the grape jelly.

So I learned to carry, along with my banding equipment, garlic, jalapeños, and other small, necessary condiments (marmalade); to hunt up the nearest shop with supplies for home-made breads, for hearty soups and stews that might arrange further futures in the field for me. I learned that while others were content to hike about excitedly scouting for hawks and shore birds, to analyze records, fetch potable water, clip net lanes—chores I had happily done for years—they considered me also working if they saw me constructively kneading bread, chopping vegetables instead of brush, searching for substitutes to put into cookies (marmalade, but *not* grape jelly).

Of course, there are mistakes—in the kitchen as well as in the field. As the other day—

"Would you add the liquid in that yellow mug to the soup kettle?" I asked a woman who was passing the kitchen counter, forgetting that a similar coffee mug held my daily medicinal dosage of potassium. Oh, well—in a big kettle of chicken broth and vegetables and barley, who is going to notice a little potassium? Butterscotch sauce for ice cream (if your quarters boast a refrigerator) looks very much like bacon grease if they have been put in similar containers and the light is dim. . . . Also, it is advisable to extract chicken feet (a flavoring trick I learned in a Central American backwater, where chickens were rare, so every inch was used) from broth before my less traveled and tolerant luncheon companions ladle these into their bowls.

"*What* are you putting into that kettle?" Joe Hickey asked me once, peering over my shoulder, scrutinizing my every move on a day when I was unexpectedly entertaining hungry professional ornithologists. His question was innocent, not critical; he had recently been widowed, he was trying to learn about cooking. But he and his eminent friends had me so flustered that I added far too much liquid to a Newburg I was attempting. I put yogurt into the kettle, too, instead of the heavy cream called for. This gave zest to what by then had become a chowder, not a Newburg at all, so I had to make biscuits to go with it instead of serving easy toast points. You improvise. You keep biscuit mix, homemade, on hand. It's easy and inexpensive; all you need to add is milk (you have to add this to store mixes, too).

What difference does it make if you add a bit too much baking powder or soda to biscuits or pancakes? None, really. Whole-wheat or buckwheat flour improves either; a little bran soaked in the liquid adds flavor; an extra egg and a shake of wheat germ turn both into a hearty breakfast. The more piping-hot oil you cook pancakes in, the crisper and more delicious—and fattening—they are. You improvise according to the circumstances and what is on your shelves.

The following recipes aren't all that great, but they are mostly nourishing. I was going to skip desserts, but people kept pressing them upon me, saying firmly that a meal without a sweet to end it is like a kiss without a squeeze. So I've added a whole section on them. They will rot your teeth. Fruit and wine are what you should have. Except for regional ingredients, these recipes are much the same whether eaten in South or Central America, the Canadian Northwest, Arizona, Florida, or New England. Many can be cooked in a very slow oven while you are out birding and will welcome you and your fellow birders with fragrance when you come in. Many can be reheated or whipped up while people shed boots and jackets, use the bathroom, pour a drink of mulled cider (that smells marvelous, too), iced tea, beer, or something more revivifying.

The recipes in this book are plain, hearty, adaptable, and often incorporate leftovers—such as scraps of last night's pasta, vegetables, meat added to the morning eggs (I've said that), as we did on Great Gull Island in Long Island Sound, where there was no refrigeration, only brackish water; where the mice were endemic and thousands of terns nested around us. Leftovers went into soup in Mexico and Tobago, into salad in the woods of Quebec.

If I don't give exact measurements, specify the size of onions and peppers, or tell you how much celery, garlic, hot pepper, carrot to use, it's because these will vary with your personal interest in color and taste and with what you have. If an unexpected car drives up to join those already parked at your door, rice or pasta, tomatoes, beans, more cheese, another can of corn or mushroom soup can be added. Few people will be critical—they are *hungry*. Usually they eat until there is nothing left.

Unfortunately, cooking takes time. Meals presuppose some Cinderella or househusband in the kitchen either a day or night or two before, if you are catering to a big group that will have been out birding on marsh or mountain. I try to honey-tongue another willing Cinderella into bringing salad. Or we stop at a fruit stand on our way home and pick up what is seasonal. Someone is always willing to chop and peel, will enjoy stir-frying while you supervise the major dish.

And, finally—this has become a pretty long introduction—I am aware that it is easier for a carload of serious birders to stop for snacks and meals at fast-food shops, then race on. It is quicker to pass out sandwiches from a brown paper bag while you set up telescopes to scan the edges of a pond or a field or a river. Serious birding is a different sport than that enjoyed by a group going out for the day who take their birding as a hobby, an excuse for an outing; to whom the conviviality of a picnic, of coming into someone's home to eat, is an integral part of the pleasure.

Now that I've warned you I'm not much of a cook, let us talk about ingredients.

Ingredients

As an insurance man, anxious to keep his clients alive and paying as long as possible, my father was interested in nutrition. He used to bring us fresh vegetables and fruit from farms along a treacherously sandy, string-straight road that he drove daily from Boston to Worcester. In those days on Massachusetts Route 9, one hay wagon could halt you for half an hour until it plodded off. Now those 40 miles are an ugly commercial strip, a dramatic example of how our world has changed.

Diets have changed, too. Our family was raised on tubs of butter and bottles of heavy cream straight from a barn; on roasts of rare beef and pork; on biscuits, pies, puddings, brownies, fruits cooked in heavy sugar syrups, jellies, fudge. My young diet-conscious friends are horrified when I detail this, but I have siblings in their eighties with minds undimmed, always globe-trotting. Fifty years from now, I wonder what health and longevity vegetarianism will have produced? I'd like to be here to see. No tobacco in our home, though; alcohol only when there were guests. No chemical sprays used on agricultural fields or orchards. Chickens scratched in the dirt for their food.

Market shelves and freezers are stacked with seductively packaged meals that are quick, convenient, bland, and expensive, and that generate trash. Birders resent a bright flick of color in a wood, a shape on a beach that turns out to be trash. They are apt to hoard their money for equipment and books, poring over maps for their next journey to some birding haven. They are aware of how much of the glamour of packages they may buy is advertising rather than food, what values they are trading for convenience. You find out a lot about people by looking at their kitchen shelves.

To save space, I will indicate to you what is on *my* shelves and in *my* refrigerator. The following are what I consider staples.

Flours—whole wheat, unbleached white (it has more gluten), buckwheat, rye; corn meal, rolled oats, bran, millet; brown as well as white sugar, molasses, honey; split peas, beans of all sorts; tomato products, celery, garlic, green peppers, carrots, onions; mayonnaise, mustard, horseradish, wine. Chocolate. No use listing more; you will find them as you go along. Nuts, raisins, coconut, yeast, spices, herbs, baking powder and baking soda. (My niece Taffy Chrisman once assembled her Special Cookies ingredients in a hurry for a party only to find that there was no baking soda on her shelves. So she repaired to the bathroom shelf, returned with Alka-Seltzer, and substituted this. There was a faintly bitter taste to the cookies, she says, but no one else appeared to notice.) Rum for use both in cooking and in a tired cook. Vanilla, cheeses, yogurt, milk, teas, coffee; cranberry and orange and apple juice; frozen lemonade, which has sugar in it (remember this if you use it as a substitute). Crackers. (I'm trying to make my own crackers but haven't yet been successful enough to please me. Mine don't break when you put cheese on them, though. They have a pleasant flavor. They are just too thick and don't keep. Store-bought ones keep for months. Why?)

Ham. When I specify *ham,* I mean real ham—baked—not those pale-pink squares from the market. Those are useful for sandwiches, though. Corned beef can be helpful as a sandwich substitute sometimes and Spam, if you are pushed, though these need to be dressed up with mustard, pickles or olive slices, sprouts, spinach leaves.

Cheese means the best you can buy for your purpose. It makes a difference.

Mustards and vinegars make a difference, too. I make my own because I enjoy it and it's easy (see "Condiments"). Also, while you can buy chili sauces, salad dressings, chutneys, jellies, and marmalades, you can make these with little effort and considerable kudos. There are recipes for them in cookbooks, if you hunt. You remodel the directions to suit yourself or as you imperfectly remember them. That's the fun. If there is extra, you can give it away in a jar attractively wrapped in a square of material. Tied with a ribbon, this doubles the gift.

Shortening. The old cookbooks specified butter, lard, Crisco, bacon grease. Their use depended on where and how you lived. Margarine became fashionable (and necessary) during World War II, when butter was hard to come by. I used to knead those darned pellets of yellow coloring into this white replacement for butter as we sat at the dinner table or I heard the children's lessons—a dull task for sure. Why did we insist on its being yellow, I wonder? Now we use butter, margarine, or vegetable oil almost interchangeably. Butter, I grant, gives better flavor, if your dish is delicate, your taste buds trained. I use margarine because it is presumed healthier than butter but mostly because it is easier to spread and to cream. Oil is even easier, but I am suspicious of its effect on textures. When we were in the woods, we used bacon grease, as our grandmothers did. I would take a 5-pound tin of Crisco, though, to make berry pies; this gives a fine, flaky crust. Perhaps our bias to our woods cooking was due to the wood stove warming our outsides on chilly mornings while my husband cleaned and fried the fish he had just caught to warm our insides and stoke our energy. Fish and muffins make a fine breakfast. Or were we just influenced by love, by the loons calling on the lake, by the pair of mergansers trailing their young past our dock? I've eaten poor meals in good circumstances and company, thought them delicious. And vice versa.

So when I say *shortening,* as I started to tell you, use butter, margarine, or oil, as is convenient, or bacon grease. Sometimes I say one, sometimes another, but it's not hard and fast.

A Birdwatcher's Cookbook

Breakfast

A lot of people—from time to time I join them—believe an adequate breakfast is juice, toast with or without butter and jam (depending on their current diet), and two cups of black coffee. Or perhaps a bowl of commercial dry cereal and half a banana.

In the homes where I ate under parental dominion, breakfast was considered the most important meal of the day, as nutritionists trumpet. We had fruit; hot cereal with brown sugar or molasses or honey, and thick cream; bacon or ham, eggs or pancakes; plus, if we still had room and time, muffins with butter and jam. The purpose of this was to provide an active body whose stomach had emptied of fuel overnight with enough energy to last through a morning at school, where we were expected to perform well; to carry us through work, either in an office or in the field, and, after I became a birdwatcher, often through a whole day because our Head Birder or Expedition Leader might not pause for lunch. (The goal of birders is a list or research; since there may be only a brief time period to accomplish this, creature comforts get ignored.)

Those of you who prefer to work on an empty stomach can

skip the following section. If you feel drained by 11:00 A.M. so you go looking for sweet rolls and coffee, don't complain to me. You will probably live as productively and as long as I will, however our habits differ. But just in case, here are a few words—or pages—on breakfast.

Cereals

Porridge is the old-fashioned word—pleasant, mouth-filling. Porridges can cook while you are dressing or skimming the morning paper, fiddling with TV news channels. They slide down no matter how hurried you are, supply you with protein, vitamins, fiber, potassium, calcium needed by your brain and body. They can be cooked with water, milk, apple juice, or syrup left over from canned fruit; with fresh or dried fruits that have been soaked overnight (apricots are marvelous); with berries, dates, raisins, sunflower or pumpkin seeds, nuts, cinnamon, coconut sprinkled on top just before serving; with yogurt, molasses, maple syrup, jam, milk, or cottage cheese. No need to be bored.

I'm talking about oatmeal, corn meal, millet, soy or wheat, with always a tablespoon of bran for fiber, and wheat germ— rich in B vitamins, vitamin E, and protein. Health-food stores offer a variety of possibilities for experiment. Dried fruits are high in potassium and iron. A tablespoon of powdered milk adds to food value and doesn't change the taste. If you "haven't time to cook porridge" (I hear you whining), the night before put a cup of whatever grain you have handy plus a spoonful of bran and some raisins or chopped apricots or apple into a wide-mouthed thermos, fill this with boiling water (leave room for expansion), shake it, and in the morning there is breakfast, warm, ready to be gulped. Or, if you are really in a hurry, you can put it in a plastic cup and eat it in your carpool as you drive to work or to the day's birding area (the days you aren't driving).

Grains should be stirred slowly into boiling liquid so that they will separate, then cooked over low heat until they are soft and chewy. If all the liquid gets absorbed, add more. One cup of water, milk, or apple juice to ⅓ or ¼ cup of grain is my basic proportion—you have to experiment some.

You can also combine ½ cup of corn meal to 1½ cups of water (and ¼ cup of soy grits, to provide protein), though this last is a southern dish, which I consider an acquired taste, although strawberry jam and cottage cheese improve it. You have to keep stirring. My grandmother called this Hasty Pudding and served it to us for dessert with lots of molasses. Probably no soy in her day. If we didn't eat enough of it at supper, she fried it for breakfast, crispy, with maple or blueberry syrup.

Millet is slow to cook but delicious with chopped apples or dried apricots stewed in, served with honey, berries, bananas, or peaches. You need to dribble millet slowly, stirring, ¼ cup into 1 cup of boiling water; it is worth the bother. If I'd have known about millet when I lived in south Florida, all those painted buntings I fed it to would have had to share with me.

Mostly I stick with oatmeal: ½ cup with 1 tablespoon of soy or rye flakes and wheat germ added, and always 1 tablespoon of bran, stirred into 1½ cups of boiling water. It's delicious with apricots you've chopped and soaked overnight. By the time I'm showered and dressed, it and my coffee are ready. I like honey in both of them. If there is any oatmeal left over, I heat it up the next day with milk and more soaked apricots.

Or—you eat breakfast 365 days a year, don't you? Oatmeal

or a poached egg on toast every day? Have you no sense of adventure?

You can combine grains and make your own Birdwatcher's Breakfast Mix. It gives your companions something to talk about, argue over, try out at home. Mix equal amounts—like 1 cup each —of oats, wheat germ, soy flakes. Sometimes I add a little millet, maybe a bit of corn meal. Brown rice, I've been told, but I haven't gone that far yet. Always, though, that cup of bran. (I put bran into everything—it adds flavor and texture.) Cook this mixture, covered, in a proportion of 1 dry to 3 wet. The liquid should be boiling, then reduced to slow heat for 20 minutes. Half an hour? Add more water, if necessary. Toward the end, toss in the day's decision of raisins, dates, or those apricots. When I dish this out, if I want I can add sunflower seeds, slivered almonds, or other nuts. A bowlful will see me through a morning's birding on a distant marsh or mountain, through the Sunday papers if it's raining, through a trip to the zoo with children if it is a family day. One winter, when I was studying birds on a mountain 75 miles from market, I would add soup to any leftovers and have a nourishing teatime warmer or supper. One young man, come down from a failed climb to the peak that rose above us, turned up his nose at this concoction, but his companion licked up every spoonful. So maybe you will like it, and maybe you won't. As I bid children, though, take three polite bites before you disdain a new food.

You can make your own granola, too. The trick is to toast the grains, well coated with a little warmed honey, vegetable oil, and vanilla, in large pans flat enough for the warm air to flow over them. Some cooks toast the oats first, for 10 minutes. Stir and scrape your pans frequently. Some directions say to toast the oats in a low oven (250°) for 15 minutes, some ½ hour, some 1 hour. I guess it depends on the size of your pan and how much you have put in it. Toast the oats *only* until they are golden brown.

KATHY FROM KEY WEST'S GRANOLA

Mix 4 cups of rolled oats with 1 cup each of wheat germ, sunflower seeds, and roasted soy beans; ½ cup each of coconut, bran, and sesame seeds; ¼ cup each of flax seeds (I skip the flax seeds and increase the bran) and powdered milk; and 1 tablespoon of cinnamon. Coat this mixture with ¼ cup each of honey and corn oil heated with ½ teaspoon of vanilla.

KITTY LARMON'S GRANOLA

Recently I have switched to Kitty Larmon's granola recipe. Kitty lives in New Hampshire, where the winter days are long, you need lots of energy. Her kitchen is sunny, its walls, cupboards, and doors covered with an accumulation from eighty years of living—children's drawings, old magazine covers, newspaper articles, cartoons, faded letters and recipes, photographs. Dried wildflowers are in jars inside on the window sills, birdseed in containers outside. I marvel at the food that comes out of this potpourri, watching her contentedly moving from stove to mixing bowl, pouring, stirring, laughing. I accuse her of liking to make granola because, like her kitchen, it has so many ingredients, all interesting. She is a measurer, with a mind as tidy as her handwriting. She gives the bounty of her spirit as lavishly as her food.

Melt ¼ pound of butter in a large skillet. Mix in and cook

over medium heat until "toasty" 2 cups of rolled oats and 2 cups of rolled wheat or rye. (I'm not sure what rolled wheat is. I use wheat flakes from a health-food store, where I get the other ingredients, too.) Remove the skillet from the heat, and add ¼ cup of maple syrup, 2 cups of sunflower seeds, 1 cup each of bran, wheat germ, coconut, and sliced almonds, less of sesame seeds. Spread this in 2 large flat pans, and bake it for 30 minutes in a low oven (250°), scraping, and checking toward the end because your oven will be different from hers. Let the mixture cool thoroughly. It will keep in glass jars for at least a month at room temperature. It needs no sugar but welcomes fruit or berries.

Pancakes

The above are healthy breakfasts, what you can eat single or family style. But what if your house is full of birders starting out on one of the "Big Days" a—Christmas Count, a Census?

The Owlers, who will be stirring before 4:00 A.M., can be pushed out the door with thermoses of coffee, with apples, bananas, granola bars, and—because someone will surely have brought them—the ubiquitous doughnuts. Small loaves of any of the medium-quick, medium-sweet breads made with nuts or raisins or dates, bananas or cranberries, even zucchini will be appreciatively received by sleepy hands. One man insists on apple pie, but he brings this himself from a bakery; I haven't time to spoil him.

This early crew will return at a reasonable breakfast hour, hungry for eggs and toast, not refusing ham or muffins. They have a full day yet ahead of them, but they need a short time for rest and recuperation, to recount their misadventures, to absorb lots more coffee with sugar and cream. If you like the group well enough, you can take from the warming oven platters of the pancakes you have made. If you have raised sons and grandsons, fed your husband's fishing friends, you also have learned to keep some batter for the men now standing in your kitchen to pour and flip and place with a flourish on a plate. Males aged five to seventy-five, in my experience, enjoy showing off their flipping skills.

Like porridge and the muffins to which we will shortly come, pancakes come in variety. I'll offer you a few.

GRANDMOTHER'S TOSS-ON PANCAKES

Marion was raised on a farm with more children than money, where corn meal and molasses and the asparagus her father grew were staple diet items. When I've attended Trustees' Meetings at the Wetlands Institute in south Jersey, I've stayed with her under orders not to notice that she has shoved everything under the big old bed in order to turn her workroom into guest quarters. Emerging sleepily mornings, I find her already at the stove flipping her version of her grandmother's pancakes.

Scald 1 cup of corn meal in enough boiling water to make mush. (You pour the water from a teakettle—there is no hard and fast measurement.) Add a dab of butter, a spoonful of honey or molasses, an egg, ½ cup of flour, 1 teaspoon of baking powder, and milk to thin the batter. Since Marion is modern and lives near a health-food store, she uses whole-wheat flour and tosses in my choice of pumpkin seeds, chopped brazil nuts, or almonds. (I suspect in her childhood what they had only were pumpkin seeds.) While the cakes cook in her grandmother's heavy oiled skillet, she drops a bit of butter on each and sprinkles the pancakes with sesame seeds. I may have as many of these good round stuffers as I want (and more than I need) served hot from the pan before we take off for our meeting.

SAMUEL WHISKER'S PANCAKES

These are more traditional pancakes, which a granddaughter learned early to make for me. She insists on serving them without, she sniffs, "all those health-food trimmings." The recipe is standard.

To ¾ cup of white flour she adds ½ cup each of whole-wheat flour and corn meal, 2 teaspoons of baking powder, 2 teaspoons of sugar, ½ teaspoon of salt, ¼ teaspoon of nutmeg (very important, Samuel says), 1 egg, 2 tablespoons of oil, 1 cup of milk. Beat the batter until it is creamy, cook the pancakes on a lightly greased griddle. Samuel makes about 12 4-inch cakes, preferably with blueberries or chopped apple incorporated into them.

KIM'S ADIRONDACK FLAPJACKS

An Adirondack lodge was part of my life for many years. Dawns, I would quietly follow trails to where warblers sang in treetops, deer regarded me from meadows, wood ducks were gathered in quiet eddies in a brook. If it was a weekend, when Kim was home from school, I would come in to her flapjacks—obviously the delight of a teen-ager, though possibly not your and my idea of what dictionaries define as "griddlecakes."

In her mother's largest bowl, she claims to put (I've never had the courage to watch; besides I am out with my binoculars trying to work up an adequate appetite) 2 cups of melted margarine (oil would be simpler), 1½ cups of powdered milk, ⅓ cup each of honey and corn syrup, 2 cups each of peanuts, chocolate chips, raisins, and 9½ cups of rolled oats. (I remember her mentioning sugar, but there is no note on the card she gave me.) These ingredients are put in a pan and baked until "set." When they have cooled, she slices the produce and puts an adequate number in her ski pack. I guess teen-agers are the same everywhere; but in case you get bored with cookbook pancakes, you could try this.

YOGURT-FRUIT PANCAKES

That's enough of pancakes. Actually, usually I use *The Joy of Cooking* recipe, with buttermilk. Only the last time—

My three unexpected guests were sleeping quietly. I crept downstairs, wondering what to supply for a breakfast that would live up to their expectations. I had fresh bread. But, unfortunately, when I had left it to cool in the oven, I had turned the switch to "Broil" instead of to "Off," so while its insides were surprisingly good, its general aspect would not enhance my reputation. Pancakes. They provide occupation as well as nourishment; everyone can play. I had just tossed out my buttermilk though, unsure of how long I should keep it. Hmmm. Yogurt, one of the recipes I was reading suggested. I had 3 small cartons—no, only 2 (one had disappeared last evening)—put in the freezer last summer for an emergency. Wasn't this an emergency? Hungry young people? So—

I mixed about 1½ cups flour—1 cup of whole wheat to ½

of white, maybe a bit more (I'm not a sifter and measurer)—
½ teaspoon of baking powder, ¾ teaspoon of baking soda,
and, in a separate bowl, beat 2 eggs, both yogurts, and 2
tablespoons of oil. I forgot to put in sweetening, which I should
have. Molasses was what I had in mind—2 tablespoons. When
my guests appeared, prepared for a prebreakfast run, I ran
frozen blueberries under cold water to thaw them a little, put
the contents of my two bowls together, and regarded the result.
Thick as biscuit dough. So I poured milk lavishly into it—
certainly 1 cup, maybe almost 2—until the batter was thin
enough to drop from a spoon. There was enough to last a
week. Only an hour later there was *no* batter left—just a dis-
ordered counter with bowls, spoons, spatulas, drips, empty
plates. Cheerful smiles, everyone comfortably settling to cross-
word puzzles.

Making do, working out recipes, is a lot of fun. When they
work.

Muffins

You are going to be in the field all day with only snacks or a
minimal lunch to bring you home. You need real food—codfish cakes and beans; maybe eggs with sausage or slices of fried
ham; Canadian bacon, hashed-browned potatoes. Biscuits and
honey. Muffins, big and crusty, split, buttered, toasted, if you

wish. What kind of muffins? There are dozens, some sweet and light, some with the weight and guaranteed value of bran muffins. I usually make one of the following, depending upon whether I want them hearty, healthy, and in quantity, or sweet, or a conversation piece.

The first recipe makes enough for a large group. The dough will keep in the fridge, to be pulled out when wanted, although it never lasts the advertised six weeks—the demand is too great. These muffins stick to the ribs, travel in pockets, are good with soup or salad for lunch or supper, satisfy the day's fiber requirements.

SIX-WEEK BRAN MUFFINS

Over 1 package of bran (any kind) in a large bowl pour 4 beaten eggs, 1 cup of vegetable oil, 1 quart of buttermilk. Let this stand for 10 minutes, plus or minus, to moisten the bran, then add 3 cups of sugar. Only that's too much unless you have a really sweet tooth—2½ cups are enough, white or brown. Mix the ingredients, and add 1 teaspoon of salt, 5 teaspoons of baking soda, and 5 cups of flour—white, or half white and half whole wheat, as you wish. Sometimes I use ½ cup of buckwheat or rye flour, sometimes I add ½ cup of wheat germ. Mix the batter, and bake at 400°. Very, very good split and toasted the next day.

CORN-MEAL MOLASSES MUFFINS

In a bowl, put ½ cup each of oil, sugar, and molasses, 2 beaten eggs, 1 cup each of milk and flour, 2 cups of white corn meal (unless you like the yellow, which is gritty) mixed with

3 teaspoons of baking powder and ½ teaspoon of salt. Stir the mixture until it is just blended; bake the muffins at 350° for 25 to 30 minutes. Makes 2 dozen. If you use paper muffin cups, be sure to bake the muffins long enough, or the paper won't peel off. Sometimes it doesn't anyway. Or you could bake this in small bread tins, making 2 loaves.

FRUIT-NUT MUFFINS

For birders too impatient to ingest a whole meal, a restaurant on Nantucket made itself famous with a muffin guaranteed to appease appetite and sweet tooth, and that can be eaten in the hand as birders hurry from one lookout point to the next, telescopes at the ready. Nantucket is a small island awash with birders always in a hurry. When you read the list of ingredients, you will understand why I call these a conversation piece.

To the usual muffin mix of 1 cup of sugar, 2 cups of flour, 1 tablespoon of baking soda, and 1 tablespoon of salt are added cinnamon, coconut, raisins, grated carrots, 1 chopped tart apple, 1 cup of drained crushed pineapple, 1 cup of oil, vanilla, ½ cup of crushed cranberries, ½ cup of nuts, and 3 beaten eggs. That ought to satisfy any birder for a while. The mixture should ripen for 24 hours, but you may not be able to arrange this. Like all muffins, they can be made ahead, frozen, and reheated. Bake them at 375° for 20 to 25 minutes.

I purloined the recipe from a church cookbook one afternoon on Nantucket. I was signing bird books of my own at a party for the benefit of the church, which I felt excused my thievery. The muffins I had eaten at the restaurant were better. Each cook, I feel, adds something of her own spirit(?) character(?) that flows into the mixing bowl through the spoons she stirs with.

Biscuits

LAZY BISCUITS

My houseguests were in running shoes and shorts; the tide wasn't yet right for shore-bird watching. They sipped a little orange juice, inquired about coffee, and headed for the door. "Be back in twenty minutes," I warned them, "unless you want burned bacon. I'm making Lazy Biscuits. They're an experiment, so I want you hungry."

Any ill-ordered refrigerator like mine is apt to have leftover sour cream taking up needed space on a shelf. Not enough to be really useful. What to do with it?

I keep a jar of biscuit mix on hand—my personal Bisquick, and as easy to use: 2 cups of white flour, 4 teaspoons of baking powder, ¼ cup of powdered milk. I substitute 1 cup of whole-wheat for 1 cup of white flour, add a little wheat germ. To this standard base can be added your choice of cheese, herbs, vegetables or shredded meats, peanut butter, molasses—whatever imagination suggests. And milk—sweet, sour, or buttermilk. (The amount of shortening and liquid varies with these added ingredients. So it's wise to consult a cookbook. Sour milk and buttermilk need ½ teaspoon of baking soda.) If you are camping, you bake one large biscuit in a heavy skillet, turning it when it is brown. If you are home, paper cups save you scouring out each tin. Let the biscuits cook long enough, though, or, like the muffins, the paper won't peel off.

Because these young people have a sweet tooth and I am hoping they will split firewood for me, I'll use that 1 cup of sour cream with the basic mix, eke it out with milk, if I have to. This means using 2 tablespoons of oil instead of 4. Stir the mixture gently, press it into a ball on wax paper, roll it thin, spread it with cream cheese, brown sugar, and chopped walnuts—¼ cup or more of each—and a sprinkling of cinnamon. Shape the dough into a roll, cut it into slices, bake it in a hot oven, 425°, for 12 to 15 minutes. I should have made this last night and chilled the roll.

Biscuits are also good for lunch or midmorning birders, with a filling of cheese, or deviled ham with onions and celery chopped fine. The advantage of experimenting is that everything gets eaten. If it doesn't, you can put what's left out on the bird feeder.

Corn Bread etc.

Yesterday's Corn Bread is fine split and toasted for breakfast, but I'm saving Corn Bread for "Lunches, Hot and Quick" (see page 55). But before we start on lunches, I have one more breakfast for birders in too much of a hurry to sit at a table. It's equally good for elevenses or lunch. It was taught me by my Students in a Bus, who now travel under the more august name of Audubon Expeditions. They get their education by driving about the country studying and living in their bus at ranches, farms, fisheries, dams, Indian villages, docks, factories, absorbing the continent's cultures firsthand. If possible, they work wherever they stay, do their own cooking, learn to get along with others in all sorts of circumstances. They have come to me for seminars for fifteen years, turning up unexpectedly on my doorstep in Florida, Arizona, Maine, Cape Cod. I'm not sure what I teach them, but I love what they teach me. Embryo birdwatchers and conservationists, they wanted to contribute to this book, so here is their recipe.

BUS BREAKFAST SPREAD

Mash 3 bananas into 3 packages of cream cheese with 4 teaspoons of honey, some walnuts, and some raisins. Squeeze a few drops of lemon juice on this, and spread it on bread.

At the other end of the scale from these breakfast suggestions is a final one, not intended to be eaten in the hand! *Cordon bleu* if you do it right, as a really fabulous woman did it for us on Nantucket one fall, where a group of us were sharing a cottage, studying hundreds of migrating birds under Edith Andrews's tutelage. (Edith has thirty-five years of migration records, and I don't know how many birders she has taught.) You have to be good at poaching eggs and hollandaise scares me, but it's a wonderful breakfast to be given when you have been netting birds for two hours on a cold morning or on a rainy Sunday morning, when no one is in a hurry to start for the beaches to see what birds a storm may have blown in.

All this dish is—actually, it's simple—is an English muffin toasted with a slice of heated Canadian bacon on top, a poached egg on top of that, and hollandaise sauce poured over. It's the hollandaise that's the trick. The recipe is under "Condiments." If it curdles, you can reconstitute it. The easiest way to do this is to blend it slowly with another egg. That's what I do when my mayonnaise curdles, too.

Lunches to Go

What with telescopes, cameras, boots, rain gear, and other accouterments that must be crammed into a vehicle, there isn't much room for coolers of food. Still, an ingenious packer can fit tins of this and that into corners to bring out at crucial moments when the sport has turned discouraging or the group spreads out for half an hour in the noonday sun.

Sandwiches can be as wide-ranging as the imagination. Roast beef and ham and chicken, yes. But also banana slices with peanut butter, garlic slices with Swiss cheese, dates or olives or sprouts with cream cheese. Sprouts and avocado are messy but worth the extra napkin. Take cold meats, cheeses, tuna or chicken salad, sardines, tomatoes in a basket, and let each birder put together his preference. This saves you time and keeps the group busy, competitive. You will need mayonnaise, mustard, horseradish. Fruit is healthier than cookies, but you need cookies, too.

A picnic like this, whether eaten off the hood of a car, off a tailgate, on a beach, or on a log, brings up the subject of bread, but bread is going to need a section all its own. Later.

What I am saying is that with a little imagination, practice, you may find yourself the center of the local birders, asked on trips you would never be able to arrange by yourself.

Plastic cups are invaluable, however much of a problem to the environment. They can hold chicken or potato or other salads, coleslaw with carrots and onion or raisins, and crushed pineapple with carrots. Gazpacho or cream soups can go in them, chilled for hot days, steaming hot from the thermos in winter.

Carrots and celery cut into sticks, of course. But why not cut these fine with mushrooms and a little onion, and put them with herbs into cold pilaf or bulgur and let people spoon this into cups or dip from a communal bowl?

TABABUI AROYMEDE

On the outskirts of Paris once, we were hunting nightingales. I was disappointed; they don't sing all that much better than our mockingbirds. I was fed the above, which was simply cold cooked bulgur mixed with greens, vegetables, mint leaves, parsley, and a dressing made, my hostess said, from ½ cup of lemon juice or wine vinegar beaten with ½ cup of olive oil. With this came hard-boiled eggs that had been wrapped individually in a spinach or cabbage leaf, then baked in cream with goat cheese. Goat cheese was a staple there; one of our soft cheeses could substitute.

STUFFED EGGS

Ordinary Stuffed Eggs can be varied by using cottage cheese instead of mayonnaise. Mash the yolks with mustard, parsley, anchovy paste or curry, horseradish or deviled ham, chopped olives, chutney (not all at once). Press sprouts on top of this stuffing.

SPINACH SQUARES

These were taught me by Nancy, a Hawk Expert who drives the highways in autumn with her head tilted to the sky, seeing birds that I, with my eyes nervously on traffic, miss. Our expeditions are interesting, to say the least, as she munches on one of the squares she brings along to sustain our energies.

"They're sort of a spinach sandwich," she says, skirting a big oil truck. "Maybe a quiche without the crust. What was the shape of that hawk's head on a pole we just passed? You didn't see it?" She wanted to turn back to show it to me, but the oil truck too close behind us discouraged her. "You can't just sit there daydreaming; you have to *look*. Shapes tell you as much as colors." I had been licking my fingers, not thinking about hawks.

Thaw and squeeze dry 2 packages of frozen spinach. Mix them with 1 pound of Monterey Jack or Roquefort or mild cheese (this sounded like an awful lot of cheese to me). Add 1 cup each of milk and flour, ½ cup of minced onion, 3 beaten eggs, and seasoned salt. Bake this at 350° for 35 minutes in a well-greased, shallow pan. Since I put garlic into everything but cakes and cookies and milk shakes, when I made this I added garlic and hot-pepper flakes—I thought her recipe too bland. And it wasn't too much cheese, after all. Different kinds of cheese produce slightly different results, too.

A more elaborate version incorporates more onion, sautéed mushrooms, 4 eggs instead of 3, ½ cup of bread crumbs, 1 can of cream-of-mushroom soup, 1 tablespoon of Parmesan, some pepper and basil. Sprinkle the top with more Parmesan.

Both versions can be served hot or cold, leftovers reheated in foil.

"They are easier to eat when you're driving if they have a crust," says Nancy, "especially the second one. But that's a refinement, and the crust flakes off on your jacket—you really should be parked somewhere. It's better eaten on a Hawk Count, where you are sitting all day on a hill watching through a telescope for migrating kettles." Kettles, to Nancy, are congregations of hawks, not kitchen equipment.

Interruption: I notice that a few lines above I specify "minced onion." When I read about mincing herbs and other staples, crushing garlic cloves, I wince. Who has time for that? I "mince" my onions and garlic with a paring knife against my thumb, dropping the pieces into the oil in a hot frying pan as I do so. I mince other ingredients often by chopping them on the breadboard with whatever knife is handy. There are gadgets that help, but they have to be washed, demand shelf room. My thumb, my breadboard are handier and require no effort to wash. Maybe I should be embarrassed by my slapdash methods, but since families and guests and also my own grumbling stomach demand three meals a day, a day has only twenty-four hours, I save time however I can. Cooking isn't a hobby with me. This makes me sincerely appreciative at the dinner tables of those who *are* gourmet cooks, and so socially well received, reinvited. I like that.

POTATO OMELETS

Along the road near Barcelona in Spain, we used to buy these omelets. They were simply omelets with as much or as little seasoning as you ordered and very thin potato slices cooked with garlic and onion in olive oil. We would eat them rolled up and hot on the spot or take them to a beach for later. Spanish fast food.

LLAPINGACHOS

A mountain dish of Ecuador, these potato cakes were similar to the potato omelets, if more complicated to produce. Sautéed onion was added to mashed potato, the mixture shaped into balls and stuffed with soft cheese. These were flattened, chilled, then fried and served hot, also along the roadside, topped with fried eggs. At one small coastal restaurant, slices of fried plantain with peanut sauce were added. The cakes came with a plain lettuce salad, well dressed.

CHICKEN WINGS

Patti, who runs the bookshop on Nantucket where I thieved that good muffin recipe, likes chicken wings for picnics. She cuts off the tips (saving them for when she makes broth), stirs up a marinade, sets her wings in this anywhere from an hour to her working day (depending upon convenience), drains the wings, lays them in a shallow pan, bakes them in a hot oven until they are crispy. She was vague on how long. "Till crispy,"

she said again. "Baste them, turn them, eat them when ready—
when *you* are ready. Hot or cold. They aren't messy and travel
well." How many? "Four to a person," she said dubiously. The
man beside her laughed. Ten was his suggestion. Save any
leftover marinade for another day. She was vague also on the
marinade. Experimenting, leafing through cookbooks, I have
worked out my own, which I keep in the fridge. Combine ¼
cup of vegetable oil, ½ cup each of soy sauce and dry sherry,
2 cloves of minced garlic, 1 minced onion, 2 tablespoons of
brown sugar, a shake of nutmeg, a bigger shake of ginger or
1 tablespoon of minced fresh ginger, salt, and pepper. I use
this for beef and pork chops, sometimes substituting herbs for
the nutmeg and ginger.

Patti (we were having a fine time discussing South American food) said that they also used to take a version of Chinese
Egg Rolls for lunch in the field—pasta wrapped around a filling of nuts, olives, scallions, moistened with soy sauce and a
little mayonnaise. Sprouts go well with this. Extra filling in a
cup can have meat added to it. She is more ambitious than I
am—or had a good South American cook.

KILL HUNGER

In the pampas of Argentina, Patti carried in her pocket the
equivalent—well, more or less—of our southwestern jerky.
She—or her cook—pounded flank or round steak thin, rolled
it around a stuffing of herb-seasoned bread crumbs, slivered
carrots, celery, onion, garlic, and green peppers, tied the roll
tightly, baked it in a shallow pan with a little red wine to
keep the meat from getting too dry, then chilled it to be sliced
or just to gnaw on during the day.

Hmmmm, I thought skeptically, as I added my first attempt at this to soup. (That's the fun of cooking—it's a gamble. And that's the advantage of keeping a soup kettle handy.) Then I found that if I marinated the steak first, moistened the stuffing with a little broth or stock, added my marinade to the red wine, I had a dandy meal. It never reached the field. How long do you bake this? It depends upon the size of your roll. Half an hour?

The local name for this sustaining snack, said Patti, is "Matambre." It proved useful to their group of hikers and birders one day when their road home was blocked by machine guns during a political coup. They had a lot of waiting to do, thought it inadvisable to stroll about using binoculars and cameras to pass the time. You can put spinach leaves in the stuffing, too, she tells me, reading these pages over my shoulder, and surely oregano and cayenne. All this sounds hard to wrap (and is), but practice neatens it.

SOBRE BARRIGA BOGOTANA

As long as we are being international, here is another "hearty finger food" that can be served cold in the field or hot at home. It is perhaps a Colombian version of Matambre. I've eaten it but have not made it; it sounds like trouble. I plan to. Someday. Again, you pound a flank steak thin, marinate it overnight in garlic, onions, tomatoes, parsley, thyme, bay leaf, prepared mustard, Worcestershire or soy sauce, salt, and pepper. (It's not that this is complicated; it just takes so many ingredients!) Cover the steak with beef stock or dark beer, and cook it, partially covered, for 2 hours. Drain it, brush it with oil, roll it in bread crumbs, fit it into a shallow dish in a hot oven for 15 minutes in order to brown the crumbs. Serve it hot at home with sauce from the gravy, or chill it to carry with you.

These two are challenges. I'm going to have to try them on a small, select group of birdwatchers. Maybe my apple-pie friend.

NOONDAY-LULL DELIGHT

From nearer home, at Hawks Mountain, Seth recommends this more North American dish. I haven't tried this one either, but Seth is trustworthy. He puts it into whole-wheat pita pockets.

Combine equal parts of ricotta and tofu (soybean curd). Add enough tomato sauce to give the mixture the consistency of a sandwich spread, then chopped onion, green pepper, parsley, oregano, garlic powder, sunflower seeds (optional). After you have filled your pita pockets with the mixture, stuff alfalfa sprouts in on the top.

CHILI IN A BAG

Pita pockets are useful. They can be tidily packed with a variety of cheeses, salads, mixed vegetables; cream cheese and ham and chutney; bananas and peanut butter; coleslaw with carrots and raisins. Almost anything. The most imaginative is chili.

In the field, slit open the top of a bag of tortilla chips. Then, from a thermos you prepared at home, pour in your personal brand of chili. Eat this from the bag with a plastic spoon. Dispose of the bag and spoon. No mess. Hot and satisfactory.

Yes, I know this last isn't a pita pocket, but it's close.

To finish up with "Lunches to Go," I have a colleague, Nan, a Tern Warden working out on distant beaches, who insists that the best lunch or snack is a bagel spread with cream cheese. It fits in a pocket; it is slow chewing so it lasts a long time; you can eat it while looking through a telescope or driving without fear of dribbles on your shirt; it sticks together; if you drop it in the sand, it is easy to wipe off.

It isn't so much the food (though that will all become absorbed) as it is the social exchanges, the decisions, that bring birders' cars together. So now if what you take on trips is a peanut-butter sandwich and an apple, if you find it easier to stop along the road and buy pizza or hamburger and watermelon, don't say I haven't given you options.

Sweet Breads

These aren't really breads—they should maybe go with "Desserts" or "Muffins." (It's hard to organize a cookbook. I wanted to put "Breads" in with "Sandwiches," but that didn't work mostly because I didn't write a sandwich section. Soups should properly go with "Lunches," but since in my home they get eaten at 2:00 A.M. or for supper, that wouldn't work either. I haven't come to soups yet, but I mean to.)

Sweet breads can be made with almost anything—bananas, prunes, cranberries, apricots, oranges, peanut butter, honey, whole wheat and molasses, dates, carrots, pumpkin, with or without nuts. (I should alphabetize these.) They are quick and easy, the basic ingredients on your shelves. Because I am always looking for a way to use up the quart of buttermilk I buy for bran muffins, ricotta cake, pancakes, or spoon bread, I pretty much stick with the following. I make it with apples, apricots, prunes, or cranberries. Let my friends arrive with traditional loaves of banana and zucchini and carrot.

FOUR-FRUIT SWEET BREAD

(Not all four together.)

Cream ½ cup of sugar with ¼ cup of shortening; add 1 egg, then either ¾ cup of chopped and cooked apples *or* ¾ cup of cooked apricots, prunes, or cranberries; add 3 cups of flour (all white or half whole wheat and half white) mixed with 1 teaspoon of baking soda and ¼ teaspoon of salt; add 1 cup of buttermilk. Stir until the batter is just blended. You can also add nutmeats and grated lemon rind or orange rind. Bake the bread at 350° for 1 big loaf. I make 3 small ones for breakfasts or gifts—it takes less time. Test the loaf (loaves) for doneness with the thin tine of a fork or with a straw, if your home runs to straws (mine doesn't). Don't slice while still hot.

PUMPKIN BREAD

This sweet bread really belongs with the recipe for Pumpkin Soup, where I tell you how to use up your Halloween decorations instead of letting them rot and go to the compost heap.

I lived for a few summers on the upper floor of a boathouse in the Adirondacks. It had one big room. A swing hung from its high rafters, lake water lapped the boats below me where barn swallows nested. There was a small kitchen, so I didn't eat often in the lodge dining room; but I had made friends with the cook, making cookies for her when she was indisposed, lending my big pottery plates for festive occasions, providing flower arrangements for parties and the weekly buffets. She used to slip me hot sweet rolls (*very* full of sugar) and other tidbits, let me into the cold room where fruit was kept. She guarded her recipes. But one day, in a fit of generosity, she gave me her card for pumpkin bread (2 loaves).

Cream ½ cup of butter with ½ cup of brown sugar, 1 cup of white sugar (that's too much). Beat in 3 eggs, ¾ cup of cooked pumpkin, ½ cup of milk, 1 cup of corn meal, 2 cups of flour, ½ teaspoon each of cinnamon, nutmeg, and vanilla. Bake the breads at 350° until a straw or tine put into the loaves comes out clean.

Lunches Hot and Quick,
Brunches, Even Suppers

SOUL-FOOD CORN BREAD

If you tire of sweet breads, you can jump to other cultures. Soul-Food Corn Bread came to me from a farm family with lots of small, hungry children. I expect it was originally eaten with molasses or cane syrup. More affluent, I find it good with maple syrup, wild grape or elderberry jelly, and excellent for lunch with yellow Cheddar.

My instructions read "2 cups white cornmeal plus one-half of ⅓ cup of flour, moistened with buttermilk, thinned to the equivalent of pancake batter with water and given a pinch of soda." I don't worry about complete accuracy in measuring that "one-half of ⅓ cup of flour." I don't worry about accuracy in this at all but use (more or less) the white corn meal and flour as above, moistened with 1 cup of buttermilk thinned with about ¾ cup of water with ¼ teaspoon of baking soda dissolved in the latter. I bake the bread for about 15 minutes in a 9-inch iron skillet—that's important. Keep an eye on it. If overbaked, as mine usually is, it comes out mighty crisp, which would take those small, hungry children more time to chew on it. I don't see why chopped bacon, partially cooked, or a spoonful of minced onion couldn't be added. The above recipe is for four. If you double it, use two skillets or one big one.

JOHNY CAKE CARIBBEAN STYLE

From a cookhouse on a Virgin Island plantation come these instructions for "Johny Cake, which down there translates into Journey Cakes as they keep forever," says my informant. "They are useful filled like a sandwich with sweets [jam], fish, chicken or Mountain Chicken, the local name for frog."

Since the woman who wrote this down had difficulty, there may be other translations to make. Time for catching fish or frogs on the Islands is more readily available than education.

"For Journey Cake makings get 5 lbs of white flour, all purpose sifted: one stick of butter marjorine, 2 tableshoons [*sic*] full of Crisco shortening, 2 table shoons full of Davis baking powder, ½ shoon salt, ½ cup sugar. Add water until all is dissolved into one main dough, and put on a whide Board or table and kneed [*sic*] Always keep back some extra flour just in case that the water gets over. After everything is well kneeded cut out dough large as donuts and frie in vegetable or Wesson oil for 10 minutes until it is Golden Brown. We have it with a nice piece of fried fish or pork chops or a nice cut of steak, and don't forget a nice cup of choclate tea, and after we finish we give God thanks for a delicious meal."

I thank you, Agnes M. A. Stapleton, Whim Plantation.

SPOON BREAD

In my southern years, I accumulated half a dozen spoon-bread recipes. You have to like spoon bread, which is basically corn-meal mush. But since I am found of millet and often have leftover buttermilk, I offer the following version to luncheon guests. If they are western, I add hot peppers to the batter and chopped scallions or onion. For easterners, I use chopped bacon or bits of ham. Sometimes I serve it with a sauce of mushrooms, tomatoes, and onion briefly cooked together. Then you hardly know you are eating spoon bread.

Mix 1 cup of cooked millet (see page 29), ¼ cup of corn meal, 2 cups of buttermilk or plain milk or a combination of the two, ½ teaspoon of baking soda if you use buttermilk or ½ teaspoon of baking powder for regular milk, 1 teaspoon of salt, 2 eggs, and 2 tablespoons of oil. Bake the bread in a greased dish at 325° for about 1 hour.

LATKA

From Soul Food, let's skip to another culture. Latka is an eastern European dish, a kind of pancake. To 2 cups of grated raw potatoes or mashed potatoes add onion, 1 egg, a slivered carrot, and 2 heaping tablespoons of flour to thicken. Fry the latka, and serve it with applesauce or sautéed apples.

SAUTÉED APPLES

Thinly slice some apples, leaving the skins on, removing the cores. Fry the slices quickly in oil and brown sugar, turning them once. The redder the apple, the more effective. (Sautéed apples go well with lots of dishes, especially pork.)

SPARROW PIE

Skip to another culture.

At a Raptor Banding Station, the usual fare can be varied with cooked pigeon breasts wrapped in bacon, but this may depend upon where your supply of pigeon decoys comes from. (The starlings also used as bait to entrap migrating hawks are not recommended.) At my own banding station in south Florida, I was often brought road and window kills of birds to make into museum study skins. I found mourning-dove breasts wrapped in bacon excellent, grosbeaks tough, cedar waxwings and robins tender.

But living in an agricultural area subject to frequent chemical spraying, I needed to be sure of where my birds had been feeding. In Arizona, I was once served a Sparrow Pie by a host who assured me that the birds had been well and safely fattened on the lavish bounty of his feeders and so would be tender and healthy. House sparrows are nuisance birds, not legally protected, so you can shoot all you want. They were imported to this country in the excited expectation that they would eat insects, be a boon to agriculture. Instead they thrive not on bugs, but on grain (and backyard feeders). They spread rapidly across the country, competing with desirable native birds.

Allen was teaching a young son how to handle a gun. Sparrows are small; it takes a lot of breast to make a pie. He had rimmed the crust with unplucked birds, their beaks pointing upward. His wife was not amused—no birder she.

If Allen had been brought up in Italy, he could have turned this dish into Uccellini con Polenta, or "Small Birds on a Yellow Bed." Fry small bits of salt pork until they are golden. Then add 1 tablespoon of minced garlic, 2 tablespoons of chopped parsley, 2 crushed bay leaves, 2 tablespoons of tomato paste, ½ cup of olive oil, and salt and pepper. Set the birds, plucked and cleaned, in this, and stew them gently, uncovered, for about ½ hour. While the birds stew, make polenta, 1 pound of fine corn meal drizzled into 1 quart of boiling water. Since this rapidly solidifies, it must be stirred or it will burn on the bottom. Cook the polenta for 20 minutes, arrange it on a hot platter, perch the birds on it, pour the sauce over them, and garnish the dish with any leftover bits of salt pork. Don't invite Allen's wife.

Hearing of my venture into the culinary world, an ornithologist friend, a gourmet well known for his work with wading birds, offered me (briefly) his recipe for White Ibis Breasts.

Licking his lips, he reminded me of an expedition we had been on together in the tropics. The last few days, we had had to live off the land, on the fish, sea creatures, and an occasional bird brought to us (dead) by our native guides. But when I pressed him for forgotten details and he saw I was serious, he hastily retracted the offer, pointing out that his financial stipends depend upon his image as a conservationist. I do remember that we used coconut milk in our cream sauce and, over our meal, discussed the possibilities of Broiled Flamingo—although, fortunately, this never materialized.

SPOFFORD'S TORTILLA CHEESE ROLLS

These, like the Sparrow Pie, also come from Arizona. Be sure to use wheat, not corn, tortillas or they won't roll. Spread them with mustard, freshly grated cheese, a bit of hot sauce. Roll them, press to seal the edges, fasten them with toothpicks, and bake at 400 ° on an ungreased sheet.

Quiche

This versatile recipe base can be either Quiche in variety or a dessert reasonably entitled Impossible Pie (see page 62). (You see why I say a cookbook is difficult to organize.) The base is 2 cups of cream or milk (your choice) and 3 or 4 eggs (your choice).

This ad-lib luncheon dish feeds 4 to 6, depending upon the size servings you cut, and allows for great variety. All quiches take about 30 to 40 minutes to bake and must be served hot.

QUICHE POTPOURRI

To prepare this sturdy dish, start with a baked piecrust, homemade with either whole-wheat or white flour, or a market variety. Line this with ¾ cup of shredded Swiss cheese, then fill it with 2 cups of vegetables—raw broccoli, carrots, celery, asparagus, chopped spinach, mushrooms—whatever you wish. Mushrooms. Add ½ cup of chopped onion, 1 minced garlic clove, ½ of a sliced green pepper. You can stop here or continue with—or substitute—2 cups of cooked and chopped chicken, ham, turkey, or seafood. Cover your mix with another ¾ cup of Swiss cheese, pour over this 3 eggs beaten with 1½ cups milk, and top the quiche with a sprinkling of sesame seeds or wheat germ or both. Bake the quiche at 350° to 400° until the crust is golden brown and a knife slid into the center comes out clean.

Quiche is not for coronary cases.

For vegetarians, substitute additional vegetables for the chicken or seafood, and add an extra egg. You can eat any leftovers the following day or send them home with a friend. In this time of career singles, gifts of food always seem welcome.

MUSHROOM-CRUST QUICHE

Sauté ½ pound or more of chopped mushrooms, and mix them with ½ cup or more of fine bread crumbs. In this, put 1 cup each of cottage cheese and Monterey Jack, ½ cup of chopped onions, seasoning, and herbs, if you want them. This quiche takes 3 eggs but no milk. If you lack cottage cheese, use cream cheese softened in the mushroom juice. If you don't have Monterey Jack, use what you have. Bake in a 400° oven, as described in Quiche Potpourri.

IMPOSSIBLE PIE

This is a dessert. The base is the same as that for quiche: 2 cups of cream or milk, 3 or 4 eggs (your choice). Add ½ cup each of margarine and biscuit mix (see page 39) or Bisquick, ¾ cup of sugar, 1 cup of coconut. Blend these thoroughly, pour the mixture into an ungreased pie plate, and bake at 350° to 400° until a knife inserted into the center comes out clean.

"I never can decide," said Martha forlornly as she copied her instructions for me, "so I usually end up making a seafood or a spinach one with the mushroom crust. The men are so hungry, so busy talking, I sometimes wonder if they know what they are eating.

"I'd rather cook than chase birds all day," she added with spirit. "So what if they did see a peregrine falcon? I had a sharpshin sitting in the oak by the feeder most of the day; I got much better looks at him."

Still Lunches

BLACK-EYED RABBIT

This is for the New Year's week (haven't I told you yet that, in the South, Black-eyed Peas bring you luck if eaten at New Year's?)

Soak 1 pound of black-eyed peas for about 8 hours or overnight. (The package gives you a quicker way, but this is easier.) Cut ¼ pound or more of salt pork into small chunks, and render them in a big skillet—that means, cook them slowly until the fat has melted, the chunks are browned and crispy. Toward the end, add a big sliced onion, green pepper if you want, and cook the vegetables until the onion is tender. Remove these from the fat.

In a double boiler, melt 1 tablespoon of butter and 2 cups of good cheese; blend in 2 cups of milk (you can use a 10-ounce can of tomato soup instead of one of the cups of milk), 1 tablespoon each of flour and molasses, 1 or 2 egg yolks, a dash of Worcestershire sauce, 1 heaping teaspoon each of dry mustard and curry (or chili sauce). Stir this until it is thick. Add the peas, and heat the mixture for another 10 minutes or so (it's in a double boiler; it will keep). Serve the rabbit over toast or English muffins. If you want a heartier dish, put a slice of ham on the toast or muffin before pouring on the rabbit. And a well-fed, lucky New Year's to six of you!

TOMATO RABBIT

Melt 1 tablespoon of butter with 1 cup of grated or chunked cheese. Add 1 cup of stewed, strained tomatoes, salt, a dash of basil, hot-pepper flakes or cayenne, and cook the mixture until it is smooth. Add 2 eggs, and cook this, stirring it until it has become custardy thick. Serve the rabbit immediately over buttered toast or English muffins. (I don't see why ½ cup or more of cooked black-eyed peas couldn't be added to this on a cold January day, bringing you luck—maybe the sighting of a peregrine falcon or a goshawk.)

CHICKEN LIVERS

I use chicken livers a lot because they are quick and easy to prepare, and the dishes can be so varied. Besides, they are good for you.

If two or three or four of us come in windblown and hungry, tired of sandwiches and coffee, while the others look over my magazines and catalogues, I take a package of livers, frozen or fresh (they thaw quickly in the hot oil), sauté them with onion and garlic (or with no garlic), add up to 1 cup of tomato sauce, cook them another 5 minutes, then add ¼ to ½ cup of dry sherry, and cover the pan. You can poach an egg apiece in this, or scatter frozen green peas on top (Alice likes peas barely cooked; these come out just right). You can add mushrooms, green peppers, braised celery which you may have already cooked and saved for such a purpose. This is a dish that can go over English muffins or a slice of toast. If you want it really hearty, stir leftover pasta or rice into it—if you aren't poaching eggs. It's ready in 15 minutes. You can eat it quickly, snatch up your binoculars, and drive 20 miles to see some rare bird advertised as being on the edge of Farmer Brown's pasture. It won't be there, probably, but you have the excitement of the chase and fellowship.

ELLIE'S SAUSAGE-ZUCCHINI FRITATA

At Stinson Beach, California, on the edge of the Pacific, is a small oasis called The Sand Dollar, which caters to birders, motorcyclists, hang gliders, and just ordinary tourists driving along this coastal highway. The Dollar serves fritatas that can be eaten hot in the sun at big wooden tables or taken with you. My son and a granddaughter live on a hill above this oasis, often eat there, help with the dishes. I've had good meals with them so feel you can trust its cook, Ellie. If you are going to spend long hours a few miles north studying the famous aggregations of shore birds in Bolinas Lagoon or going on to the Pt. Reyes Bird Observatory at Palomarin, take one of her fritatas along with you. I haven't yet cooked one. It's not yet zucchini season, when friends keep me supplied—oversup-plied—with this bland squash, but I am inching toward it.

Sauté ½ pound of sausage; remove it from the pan. Then sauté in the fat 2 chopped garlic cloves, ½ cup each of chopped green pepper and onion, 1 cup of cubed zucchini. Cook the vegetables briefly until the zucchini is tender but still crisp. Beat 5 eggs with an 8-ounce package of softened cream cheese,

½ cup of half-and-half, a pinch of seasoning, and fold in 1 cup of diced or grated Cheddar. Add the sautéed ingredients, spread everything in a lightly greased 9-inch pie plate, dust it with paprika, and bake it at 350° for 45 minutes or until the fritata is set. Good hot or cold.

Zucchini may be replaced by other vegetables, lightly cooked and drained (spinach, green beans, asparagus, eggplant, mushrooms, tomatoes—ad lib); with thinly sliced pepperoni and sweet or hot peppers; with mushrooms, ½ cup of diced ham, and sweet red and green peppers. It's a versatile dish.

HOBOTEE

This is from Carolina—hearty.

Brown 2 pounds of ground beef or sausage with 2 onions and 2 tablespoons of curry. Mix this with 1 beaten egg, 1 cup of bread crumbs, 1 tablespoon of sugar, 2 tablespoons of vinegar, a few almonds, and ½ cup of coconut, and bake it. If it seems too dry, mix in a little milk. (As you may have guessed, I pick some of my recipes for their names.)

Soups

I grant that these suggestions presuppose a birder or a spouse or an agreeable companion who has been willing to stay at home stirring and baking and packing in baskets and thermoses. You do get invited to go on more trips—and more interesting ones with more interesting people—if you have a reputation for culinary surprises as well as for stamina and identification skills.

But the basic ingredient of any nourishing midday meal should be (how have I put this off for so long?) *soups*.

Soups can be hot or cold, depending on your climate and the weather. Served at noon or midnight, they stick to the ribs. Hot, they can have a raw egg drizzled in at the last minute or a handful of small chunks of Swiss cheese; they warm the hands as well as the belly, travel well in big kettles and thermoses. Cold, they can be embellished with lemon or hard-boiled-egg slices, sprouts or parsley or fresh herbs. Of value is that they can incorporate any leftovers—vegetables, meat, pilaf, barley, rice, pasta, the last spoonful of a casserole. I have a friend who adds peanut butter to his. A spoonful (of soup, not peanut butter) in scrambled eggs instead of milk does no harm.

The one way I don't use soup is plain, out of a can. That's

dull. (And incorrect, too. Sometimes I cheat. If I'm unprepared, I mix a can each of split pea and tomato soups, add a can of consommé, cream to thin, and splash in a good bit of dry sherry as I fill the bowls. If I lack cream, a dollop of yogurt can substitute as I serve it. Mushroom soup goes well with tomato, too.)

Soups of the House, Hot

If your fridge is full of bits of this and that too good to throw out, not enough for a meal, take a chicken or turkey carcass that you have saved in the freezer for this purpose and simmer it overnight—or all day—with any vegetable broths you may also have saved. Strain, chill, remove any fat. From then on, soup is creative. Add dried beans or peas to the broth; any root vegetables like parsnips, potatoes, turnips. Onions and garlic certainly (sautéed first). Squash is a fine, rich thickening for both cold and hot soups (add the water you have boiled it in; it's invaluable, as are any pasta or rice leftovers). At the end, add fresh vegetables, and simmer only until they are still crisp—carrots and peas for color, celery, broccoli, a little cauliflower. Not too much of the latter—the taste is strong.

My name for this is Peasant Soup. My friend Petruska calls hers Stout Soup, adding chunks of beef or chicken from a recent roast with the vegetables. With crusty bread or rolls to dunk into this, a green salad if it's that time of year, a glass of wine, this provides a full meal.

BLACK-BEAN SOUP

This soup is equally hearty. It takes preparation but is worth it. Make a double amount, and freeze it in containers.

Soak 2 cups of black beans overnight, and drain them. Add

water to cover—an ample amount since the beans will swell as they cook (you may have to add more). Use broth, if you have any. Simmer the beans for 3½ hours or more with that ham bone you saved from your last party. Remove the ham bone. Sauté 2 large onions and at least 4 garlic cloves in a little oil, add these to the beans with carrots, celery, bay leaf, hot-pepper flakes, a spoonful of peppercorns, 2 cloves, salt, a dash of red-wine vinegar (or wine—½ cupful of this), tarragon, and continue to simmer. This is soup, keep it adequately liquid. If you want a really thick soup, a meal in itself, toward the end thicken it with millet or barley or rice or pasta or, at the very end, with bread or corn-meal crumbs. (You can use turkey stuffing if you don't have any of these.) Then you decide whether to run all this through a blender or just mash the beans up some and serve the mixture as it is. Add a good tablespoon of dry sherry or red wine to each bowl. More if the bowls are big. More if you have blended it to carry into the field in a thermos. Serve it—hot or cold—with corn or French or rye bread, with cheeses and salad. If you used jalapeños, you had better also have beer on hand.

CUBAN BLACK-BEAN SOUP

This calls for more garlic, really hot peppers, and more wine, but is otherwise the same as the preceding recipe. For nutritional balance, both can be served (hot) over rice.

COUNTRY-SUPPER SOUP

(Although the recipe is for 10, it is expandable.)

I am giving you all my hearty, full-meal soups first, then we can taper off. If you make this, you should thank a very gracious lady, Marie Aull of Aulwood, Dayton, Ohio. Her Aulwood Wildflower Garden and Conservation Farm are famous. She fed this soup to our National Audubon Board at a meeting there. We were going out to watch, or had just come in from watching, the mating flights of woodcock in her meadow. I have used it many a time and leave her directions unchanged. You don't gild a lily.

Sauté ½ pound of lean sliced bacon, chopped, and set it aside. To 2 cans of condensed onion soup, 1 20-ounce can of solid-pack tomatoes, 1 cup of diced potatoes, ½ pound of diced zucchini, 1 clove of garlic, minced, 1 small bunch of parsley, chopped, and 1 bay leaf, add 9 cups of water, generous pinches of thyme, marjoram, and basil, salt and pepper to taste. Bring the ingredients to a boil, then simmer the soup for 1 hour. Add 2 cups of broken, uncooked spaghetti, 1 cup each of diced carrots and celery, 2 packages of frozen lima beans. Cook the soup 30 minutes longer. Just before serving, add the reserved bacon, ½ cup of grated Parmesan, and a dash of Madeira to each bowl. Serve the soup with crusty hard rolls or big crusty muffins, and salad.

LENTIL SOUP

This hot soup is quick and easy. It can be vegetarian or have bacon, cooked sausage, shredded ham, or other meats added to it.

Cook the lentils according to the directions on the package (for about 20 minutes) with onion, garlic, celery, bay leaves, herbs, and either an 8-ounce can of tomato sauce or a large can of tomatoes (it's the color and flavor you want). Toward the end, stir in carrot coins, green peas or beans, okra or limas, any leftovers in the fridge that seem suitable. Add ½ cup of wine vinegar or red wine (more of the wine), and correct the seasonings. Serve this with a loaf of French bread hollowed out, filled with cheese, and heated; or cold, filled with sprouts, shredded lettuce, and cheese.

SQUASH SOUP

A day comes each November when storm blows a glowing golden carpet of pine needles onto my steps, swirling them about the pumpkin and squash I had set out for Halloween. It is time to bring these in and transmute their warm, decorative colors into something warm and decorative for the inner woman and whatever men may stop by. The same recipe works for both squash and pumpkin and may be served either hot or cold.

Sauté 1 or 2 onions; add 1 or 2 tablespoons of flour for thickening, then 3 cups of chicken broth or milk, and 4 cups of steamed and puréed squash or pumpkin. (Steam them cut up, seeds and fibers removed, skins on. When they are soft, the skins come off readily.) Season this with salt, pepper, ½ teaspoon of ginger, 1 tablespoon of brown sugar, a shake of cinnamon. Add slivers of red and green pepper for color (these don't need to be cooked). Add shredded ham or chicken if available, croutons if not.

I also use squash and pumpkin like zucchini, as a thickener in casseroles or stews, and in Tamale Pie (see page 105). They add texture, a bit of taste, are good in any soup. I save the water they steam in.

Any leftover pumpkin from Halloween I freeze to use later in Pumpkin Bread (see page 53) or Pumpkin Pie (see page 190).

LIGHT BARLEY SOUP

I made barley soup for a girl once in her tiny New York room that had only a hot plate for cooking. I had brought a store package of barley with herb-and-vegetable mix in it. We added 1 can of chicken broth, 1 cup of water, and, at the last minute, 1 package of frozen peas, and just heated it through. I thought surely there would be enough for a second meal for her, but it had been a long time since she had eaten anything like that and then her roommate arrived . . . Barley makes a good soup base.

Cold Soups for Summer

The above are winter soups. The following are summer soups that can be whirled up in a blender, chilled, to eat at table or to put into big thermoses for bird trips.

BIRD-CLUB ZUCCHINI BISQUE

I specify zucchini here because my gardening friends always have zucchinis to donate. But the recipe may be used for other vegetables, doubled or tripled as wished.

Combine 2 cans of chicken broth or its homemade equivalent with 1 cup of water, 2 cups of sliced zucchini, ½ cup of chopped onion, 3 tablespoons of wheat pilaf or rice, 1 tablespoon of curry, ½ teaspoon each of ground ginger and dry mustard, salt, and pepper. Simmer this, covered, until the rice and zucchini are tender, blend it, then stir in 1¼ cups of milk, and chill it. Serve it garnished with a dollop of yogurt and some chopped dill or parsley or both.

There are excellent Portuguese soups made with kale, but my friends seem nervous about kale and unsure of what chouriço and linguiça are. So I am not including them.

AVOCADO (OR CUCUMBER, BROCCOLI, SPINACH, ASPARAGUS, OR GREEN-PEA) BISQUE

In south Florida, where avocados and limes dropped from grove trees along the edges of our country roads, my neighbors and I used to make a fine free cold soup by blending a good-sized avocado (they can weigh up to 2 pounds, are smooth, delicious, and abundant) with cold chicken broth, 1 to 2 teaspoons of lime juice, 1 cup of heavy cream, and salt to taste. Serve it with a sprinkling of minced chives or parsley.

In the North, this can be made as simply with cucumbers. Or with broccoli, spinach, asparagus, green peas. I'm apt to blend in a bit of celery, garlic, and onion with these. The bisques are equally good hot, with biscuits and honey for lunch.

GAZPACHO

This is merely any or many of the above vegetables blended with tomatoes—ad lib—herbs, and strong seasoning. I use V-8 juice and chicken broth, add sour cream, let the blend stand overnight. Sometimes you need to strain it, get the tomato seeds out. Like the other soups, a garnish of croutons looks nice and gives a tasty crunch.

BEET SOUP (BORSCHT)

I was a long time finding a recipe for Beet Soup that pleased me, but finally I did—on a picnic in a New Hampshire meadow. Two of us were watching a loon nesting on an artificial island—the young were due to hatch. I should have tatooed my companion's name on my arm, I was so grateful to him; but worrying about his insistence on the pickles I had forgotten to pack, I forgot this. Not his recipe, though. It doesn't make much; he had doubled it. And it is well to carry your hard-boiled-egg slices separately (and carefully).

Blend 1 16-ounce can of beets with 1 16-ounce can of tomato juice, 3 tablespoons of chopped onion, 1 minced garlic clove, and 3 small dill pickles. (I hate dill pickles, but that's what makes this soup—that and the drop or two of Tabasco or other hot-pepper sauce you put in when no one is looking.) My illustrator for this book can't eat garlic and is apprehensive about hot peppers. It's a measure of my affection that I make a special thermos of this just for her, but she doesn't know what she is missing.

If you serve this at home, add a dollop of sour cream and a sprinkling of chopped dill on top of the hard-boiled-egg garnish. If you are taking it into the field to serve in cups, blend ½ cup of sour cream and the dill with the rest. By the time the egg slices are unwrapped, they will have crumbled. But that's all right—they look nice on top and are a necessary ingredient.

74

BLOODY MARY SOUP

And, finally (it would be final for me, anyway), I have a friend who hikes with her father in Acadia National Park in Maine. He demands that the soup they take along in big-mouthed thermoses be hot—warming in more ways than one. Hearing of this book, claiming to be birdwatchers, too, they insisted I include this recipe.

Sauté celery, sweet red pepper, and 1 or 2 jalapeños. Add to this 4 cups of tomato juice, 2 cups of drained tomatoes, 3 tablespoons of horseradish, salt, pepper, 1 or 2 slices of lemon or lime. Blend this, stir in 1½ teaspoons of caraway seeds, 3 tablespoons of Worcestershire sauce, and a dash of sherry pepper sauce. Heat, add 1 cup of vodka, and ladle the brew into a thermos—citrus slices and all. And a little dill.

"How much celery and peppers?" I asked.

"Oh—enough. Whatever you want. Same goes for the vodka, too."

So there you are, suit yourself. I have friends who would definitely leave out the jalapeños, but the amount of warmth here is, again, up to you.

Meats

Since often you find vegetarians among your guests, I suggest you divide your stews and casseroles (and soups) into separate dishes and also into hot and bland, carefully marked, since easterners are not always happy with jalapeños and Tabasco. This means two casseroles to wash later, but it makes for more comfortable friends, which is more important. Raised a Yankee, I often omit salt pork from my southern dishes, so I forgive those whose taste buds are not conditioned to Mexican and southwest spices.

Meats

POT ROAST I

I have a daughter-in-law who, in spite of my efforts, divides all birds into two categories by size—chickadees and gulls. She also believes in cooking when she gets home from work, but not if it takes any real time. We don't speak the same bird or kitchen language! Unfortunately for my self-esteem, she turns out excellent meals in about one-eighth the time I do; her family is obviously satisfied and healthy. One of her favorites, which she invites me to share because you don't cook it if you live alone, is pot roast.

"Simple," she says, perching in my kitchen, watching me stir and strive. "You place a roast on a big sheet of foil, empty a can of tomato sauce and an envelope of onion-soup mix over it, wrap it, and set it away in a slow oven for four hours while you go birding. Or a three-hundred-degree oven and stay as long as you wish."

Simple, indeed!

Actually, you can go birding while any roast or fowl cooks, if you put it in a low oven, the temperature of 250° or 300° regulating your free time.

POT ROAST II

This version is from Vermont, from a group that had been out working on the State Bird Census. Pot roast is better the second day, better still if enough red wine has been added to it. There are many variations.

Cook the roast long and very slowly in a covered kettle with

1 undiluted can of mushroom soup and that useful onion-soup mix (1 envelope) sprinkled over the meat. Potatoes and carrots can be put in or cooked separately and added later. (I don't see why a kettle isn't as easy as, or easier than, wrapping in foil.)

RED-FLANNEL HASH

With any leftovers from the pot roast, the next day you can make Red-Flannel Hash. Moisten them with cream or tomato juice, and bake in a skillet for 40 minutes. I'd add more potatoes and onion, as in a proper hash.

ROAST LAMB

Onion-soup mix is obviously standard with beef. It comes to me in many recipes from friends—in stews, casseroles, soups, or with ground beef mixed with noodles or rice or pilaf. It isn't applicable, though, to an equally simple dinner of roast lamb.

Several hours before serving, Jeannette paints hers with a paste made of ¼ cup of good mustard, 2 tablespoons of soy sauce, 1 mashed garlic clove, 1 teaspoon of thyme, and ¼ teaspoon of ginger. Whisk 2 tablespoons of olive oil into this "by droplets," she says severely, knowing my hasty ways. A 6-pound roast she cooks at 350° for 1¼ hours for rare, 1½ hours for well done, and asks Paul Brooks to carve it. (That's how I can include this in *A Birdwatcher's Cookbook*—Paul is an eminent naturalist. Jeannette is on good terms with the cardinals and woodpeckers, the chickadees and titmice at her feeders, but at heart I think she is more of a stove watcher. She certainly feeds her friends well.)

WILD RICE

This will take the same timing; you can bake it in the oven with the lamb.

My nephew supplies me with it from his plantation in northern California. (I had thought rice plantations were all in Georgia or the Carolinas). He tells me this black gold provides twice or more the protein of its brown or white cousins; is far higher in things good for you such as iron, thiamine, riboflavin, niacin; is also rich in potassium, phosphorus, and other B vitamins. Since he is a rangy six foot two, a champion sailor, a mountain man, a demon gardener, and has five children, maybe eating wild rice is smart to do. I like it for its taste. It is good in soups, stews, seafood salads, muffins, pancakes, omelets, under stir-fried vegetables.

His wife Taffy's fail-safe method of cooking it with other dishes she may have baking (like lamb) is to put 1 cup of wild rice and 3 cups of chicken broth in a casserole in a 350° oven. This given her time to walk along the river and see what shore birds may be there.

PORK CHOPS WITH WILD RICE AND APPLES

This is my favorite wild-rice recipe.

Brown pork chops in an electric frying pan (or a heavy skillet with a cover) in a small amount of oil. Remove the chops, sprinkle 1 cup of wild rice in the pan, set the chops back on this, spread with onion slices, pour over 2½ cups of chicken broth, and simmer covered, for about 1 hour or until the rice is cooked. Top with apple slices with their colorful red skins left on, and simmer again for another 15 minutes.

I can get only 4 chops in my pan, which limits my guests. If you have more meat, increase the recipe accordingly. (Although, as my friend Eleanor points out: "If you have only four for dinner, *you* get a chance to talk.")

PORK CHOPS WITH BEANS

A similar dish from a Virginia plantation.

Spread baked beans in a pan, and set pork chops on top. Cover them with mustard, brown sugar, a bit of catsup or chili sauce. Bake for about 1½ hours, depending on the thickness of the chops. Garnish with sliced onion or lemon, and serve this with relishes, green salad, and crusty bread.

In some modern cookbooks, catsup is called ketchup. I have been told the original name derived, in some mysterious fashion, from the Chinese. *The Joy of Cooking* tells us that the condiment originated in Malaysia, its name coming from the native word for "taste." Dictionaries accept both spellings. It is a combination of tomatoes, peppers, garlic, onions, and a variety of spices which are boiled down, strained, then thinned with vinegar and boiled again. The recipes for chili sauce are similar, but the mixture is not strained.

SHIPWRECK SURVIVORS

Combines both rice and beans; can be used with pork chops or ground beef.

Layer thinly sliced potatoes over thinly sliced onions. Add

browned pork chops or a thick layer of ground beef, a thin layer of raw rice, chopped celery, 2 cups of drained canned kidney beans, 2 cups of tomatoes or catsup or thinned tomato sauce. Bake the chops, uncovered, in a slow oven, adding more liquid if needed. The recipe doesn't call for red wine, but I expect the sailors would prefer it to replace at least part of the tomato liquid.

ROAST ARMADILLO

I wish I'd had this recipe when I worked at Archbold Biological Station in central Florida one winter. There were armadillos all over. A researcher had brought some in to study and had not removed or roasted them when he finished his thesis. They multiplied. Other years in south Florida, I had eaten possum and raccoon that preyed upon my hen yard. I would gladly have decimated the abundant armadillos that dug up any flowers I planted—even my doorstep pots—trying to make my small quarters at Archbold a home. Those darned critters dug up everything, rustled in the bushes along paths I walked at night, scaring me. The fire-alarm system in my cottage wailed if I even singed a piece of toast or a visitor smoked his pipe, so I learned early not to cook bacon and pork chops, but to subsist on tuna and cold chicken. If I had known armadillos were edible . . .

Diane Weyer of Belmopan, Belize, provided this recipe. The animals uprooting her gardens there were tapirs, not armadillos. I'll have to find out if she ever cooked tapir stew. Or paca. She doesn't answer letters; the Belize postal service eats them, maybe.

Put ½ a cleaned armadillo (it is a common meat in Belize) in a roasting pan with ½ inch or so of water and some salt.

Cover the pan, and roast the meat until it is cooked through but *not* tender. (I don't know how you tell this; it would depend on the size of the animal. I can't advise you.) Diane uses an oven temperature of 450° but says some use 300°. Remove the cover, and add more water to the pan, if it is needed. Stick about 1 dozen cloves in the roast, sprinkle it with white pepper to taste, and smear it thoroughly with honey. If you want to be fancy, you can put peach halves or pineapple slices on top. Continue cooking it until it is very tender. Use lots of red wine. If I get back to Belize (or Archbold), I'll try to work out more explicit directions.

Stews

There are as many ways of making stews and chilis as there are cookbooks, geographical locations, and whims of iron, so I will be brief and leave you to experiment. You can't go very wrong.

Basically, Stew is meat—beef, lamb, goat, rabbit, buffalo. (Kidneys are a different dish. A visiting English birder will be glad to advise.) The meat is cut up, seared. Some cooks roll it in flour, some don't. It should stew slowly—which gives you all day to go on a birding trip (you can regulate the time with a liquid of vegetable stock, tomato juice, water, and, by all means, some red wine). Root vegetables like potatoes, onions, garlic, carrots, celery, kohlrabi, parsnips, turnips can be added. Herbs, seasoning. The liquid should be thickened with a flour paste (or corn meal or bread crumbs) at the end, more liquid added as needed. The more liquid, the more gravy but the less flavor in the meat. Okra thickens and enhances a stew, too, but that is my southern living showing. It's hard to sell okra to New Englanders or to find it in their markets.

CLASSIC STEW

Brown 2 pounds of beef-chuck cubes; add salt, 1 onion, several celery stalks, 5 carrots, all chopped; 1½ cups of tomato juice, 1 tablespoon of sugar, 2 tablespoons of Minute tapioca or barley, herbs. Cover the pot, and cook in a 250° oven for 5 hours. It can be stirred midway, if anyone is home, and more liquid added; but if the oven temperature is very low, this won't be necessary. Don't forget the red wine. Try adding parsnips.

HIGH-PLAINS STEW

Buffalo meat is more glamorous than beef. Cook it, cubed, uncovered, in a heavy skillet in oil or bacon drippings until it has lost its pink color—about 20 minutes. Then sauté onions and garlic (lots) in the oil, and blend in ¼ cup of mild chili powder, 2 tablespoons of cumin, oregano, paprika, salt and pepper to taste. Pour 3 cups of tomato juice, 2¼ cups of beef broth, 1 cup of brewed coffee or red wine over the ingredients. Simmer for however long you wish (2 hours at least), and at the end throw in pinto beans that have previously been soaked and cooked to just tender.

GOAT STEW

To many people this is frightening, but goat makes a fine, rich dish. Be sure your goat is young, though, and marinate it in red wine for at least a day. Then proceed as in other stews, with vegetables and, if your taste runs that way, hot peppers or pepper flakes.

POLISH LENTIL STEW

Like the others, this stew can be prepared ahead and reheated. Cook 1 cup of lentils, salted, for 20 minutes or until they are tender. Add 3 garlic cloves and 2 onions that have been chopped and sautéed in oil, 1 bay leaf, herbs, and a 20-ounce can of tomatoes. Cook this until the liquid has mostly evaporated, then mix in 2 to 3 pounds of sausage that has been removed from its casing (if any) and cut into 1-inch slices. Season and bake for 30 minutes. If it is dry, add tomato juice.

COLD NIGHT'S LAMB STEW

This dish comes from the Executive Director of the Massachusetts Audubon Society, a man certainly high in the hierarchy of birdwatchers. He used to be a professional cook, which shows how one career can progress into another, if you leave yourself open.

Brown 2 pounds of lamb cubes well, then simmer them for 1 hour in ½ cup of vegetable stock and ½ cup of tomato juice. Add turnips (turnips are essential to this dish) and carrots, simmer another ½ hour, then add 1 to 2 packages of frozen lima beans or 1 or 2 cups of cooked black-eyed peas. If you use the peas, you won't need rice or potatoes to dish the stew onto (but that is a matter of choice—you can have both).

GREEK STEW

Brown 1 pound of lamb, chunked, and 1 sliced onion in ¼ cup of oil for 10 minutes. Add 2 packages of frozen okra (see my previous comments on okra in New England), 1½ cups of stewed tomatoes, ¼ cup of wine, salt, and pepper. More wine, if you wish. Cover, and simmer this for 1 hour.

MADI'S STEW

I had expected a really exotic recipe from Madi Tate in Louisville. She had been to China and Russia since last she fed me sandwiches in her garden with a beloved Tante Louise, who used to feed me in India in *her* garden. What did I get? Stew!

"The birdwatchers I know are so busy chasing birds, they can't take time to cook," she wrote. "This is easy, delicious, and will cook while you are out." That's what everyone tells me about stews, and, of course, it's true.

Mix 4 pounds of stew meat (she doesn't say which kind, but I presume beef) with 1 package of onion-soup mix, 1 can of mushroom soup, as many fresh mushrooms as you like, 2 packages of frozen little green peas, and cook the stew in a covered casserole for 3 hours in a 325° oven. Eat it hot, or, when it cools, refrigerate it, and reheat it 2 or 3 days later, if you wish. No further seasonings. What? No garlic, oregano? No okra? No. She likes it over noodles or another pasta. The peas go in at the very end.

(I'm not much on pasta. We had to live one summer in an Italian hospital caring for a desperately ill child. Heaping dishes of plain pasta seasoned with emotional stress were our noon and evening meals. I developed a prejudice against it. Also, I dislike watching people eat spaghetti or noodles, the long strings trailing from their forks or mouths. Now there are dozens of more aesthetic pastas, all evidently good. They make a fine, nourishing meal if served with a healthy amount of cheese— good cheese—or with a tangy vegetable sauce. I'm just biased.)

FRUIT STEW

Adelle Davis, in her book *Let's Cook It Right* (New York: Harcourt Brace, 1947), recommends a fruit stew with prunes, pineapple, apples, curry, raisins, peaches or other fruits, pre-served ginger added to the browned meat instead of herbs and vegetables. I haven't had the courage to try this on my birding friends yet, but I'm inching toward it. Maybe a Ladies' Lun-cheon?

NEW ZEALAND CURRY

This is a sort of stew.

Sauté 2 sliced onions. Add 1 chopped apple, 2 sliced bananas, 3 chopped tomatoes. Stir these; don't let them brown. Then add chopped beef (my instructions don't say how much), 2 tablespoons of curry, a pinch of sugar, lemon juice or wine, 2 tablespoons of chutney, 3 tablespoons of raisins, coconut, and salt. Cover, and simmer the curry until the meat is tender. The birders who took me out in New Zealand seemed quite normal and not undernourished.

Chilis

Chili is served, with good reason, wherever hungry men and women come in from heavy outdoor work. It can be made in large amounts, kept for days, even frozen. The red kidney beans, drained, should be added at the end. Chili can be made from beef, pork, venison—shank, chuck, or shoulder, cut into cubes. If the final result is greasy, corn meal can be added to sop this up. Chili powder should be unseasoned and stored in airtight containers. Toasted cumin seeds can be used generously.

CLASSIC CHILI

This version calls for 2 large onions, sliced and sautéed, then added to 1½ pounds each of venison and pork cooked with 2 teaspoons of salt until the meat is no longer pink—

about 20 minutes. Skim off the fat, add ⅓ cup of chili powder. (There are as many kinds of chili powder as regions. Some are mild; many burn an unaccustomed throat. It pays to experiment.) Add 3 tablespoons each of cumin, oregano, and cocoa (yes); 2 tablespoons of cinnamon, cayenne to taste, 4 cups of tomato juice, 3 cups of beef broth. Bring this to a boil, then simmer for about 1 hour. Taste, correct the seasonings, simmer 30 minutes longer. Stir in 8 cloves of minced garlic (yes), 2 cans of drained red kidney beans, then thicken the chili with corn meal, if needed. Beer, a strong red wine, or a crisp white one goes well with this.

HOT CHILI

Cook 3 pounds of ground beef and 1 pound of hot sausage. Add 3 onions, sliced and sautéed with 4 minced garlic cloves, 2 or 3 large cans of tomatoes, 1 teaspoon each of oregano and brown sugar, bay leaves, salt, 4 tablespoons of chili, and ½ cup of dry wine (more in my home). Simmer this over very low heat for 4 hours. About 20 minutes before serving, add 3 cans of drained kidney beans. If additional guests show up, put more beans in the chili and more beer on the table. Serves 12 to 15.

VEGETARIAN THREE-BEAN CHILI

For purists, this can be made with water instead of meat stock; or use vegetable stock. It is better cooked 1 day ahead. The recipe claims to serve 8, but I'd take that with a grain of salt. The writer wasn't thinking of birders.

Soak ¾ cup of coarse bulgur in 1 cup of orange juice. In ⅓ cup of oil, cook 2 sliced onions, 8 minced garlic cloves, 3 tablespoons each of cumin and oregano, 1½ teaspoons of thyme, 1 to 2 teaspoons of cayenne, ½ teaspoon of cinnamon. (You might try cocoa in this, too—a spoonful.) Cook the mixture, stirring, for 5 minutes. Add 1 35-ounce can of Italian plum tomatoes, cut up, 3 cups of beef, chicken, or vegetable stock, or water, 2 or 3 tablespoons of chili, 3 tablespoons of salt, 1-pound can each of red kidney beans and garbanzos (chickpeas), drained. Cook this over low heat for 30 minutes, stir in the bulgur, add 2 medium zucchinis, shredded, ½ pound of green beans, 2 large sweet peppers, cut up. When the green beans are crunchy, add 1 pint of sour cream and more liquid, if needed. Hot peppers can be used according to taste.

CHILI CHÈVRE

Fill oven-proof bowls with Vegetarian Chili, crumble 2 ounces of goat cheese (or soft cheese) over each bowl, and broil for a few minutes until the chili is bubbling and the cheese browning. Garnish each bowl with tomatoes, sprouts, scallions, diced avocado, and big chowder crackers (if you can find them—I can't).

Note: Either of the above vegetarian chilis can be served in a pan or casserole topped with dollops of corn-bread dough and baked for 20 minutes. Or they can be topped with cooked pasta, rice, or potatoes dusted with cheese. Or with tacos. French fries were suggested once, but not in *my* home!

CHILI OMELET

This is a good breakfast or lunch.

Break an egg on top of a bowl of chili, and bake the chili until the egg is done.

Note: For any group, it is kinder to make your chili not too hot. Set out hot sauces on the table; they can be added by aficionados.

BOATHOUSE SPECIAL CHILI

This is hearty, but the Boathouse Boys have been out on the water all day and are hearty, too. They like to cook.

In hot oil, brown 1½ pounds (or more) of beef. Add 1½ cups of sautéed onions, 1 can of *undrained* kidney beans (that doesn't sound like enough; I'd think 2), 1 can of drained solid-pack tomatoes, taco sauce, 3 tablespoons of chili powder, 1 can of black olives. Ground beef will cook quickly; chunks of stew or shank beef take longer. The Boys layer the above in a pan with grated Cheddar (not too much) and tacos or corn chips, then layer again. This bakes for about 45 minutes, while they are working on their boats or drinking beer. They top their helpings with sour cream and shredded lettuce.

Or you can drain the beans, replacing the liquid with ½ cup of peach juice and ½ cup of strong coffee (rum, say the Boys), 1 bottle of chili sauce, and ½ bottle of catsup. For warmth, anyone may add more taco sauce. Usually someone has a wife whom he has persuaded to provide cheesecake. This gives them strength to go birding another day.

Chicken

As a lecturer visiting here and there about the country, I get my share of chicken. I never tire of it, no matter how it is cooked. At home, I roast it, eating every scrap of the crisp herbed skin (not on a dieter's menu—but, then, neither am I). I get a lot of mileage out of a chicken—salad, sandwiches, eventually soup. The second time round, I like it best in a casserole with rice, lots of mushrooms, and a delicate seasoning that not too many of my hostesses achieve. (Men seem to prefer to fry or grill their chickens; they don't give me casseroles.) I have no firm recipe for mine. Sometimes it has wild rice in it, always a bit of onion, a hint of garlic, of soy sauce. I suppose, basically, it is cut-up chicken, rice, seasoning, and cream-of-mushroom soup. Sour cream, a bit of ginger or curry or both. My advice is to experiment. I've been given it with broccoli—not too much—in it, with a light topping of herb dressing. Run your casserole under the broiler at the last minute to toast this. I like it every way.

A neighbor arrived at my door one noon with a decorative chicken dish, hot rolls, and currant jelly. I was just home from the hospital without strength enough to stir up anything more than soup or toast in my kitchen. When, on another day, I asked her how she had made the casserole, she gave only a secretive smile. It was perhaps a version of Chicken Kiev— broccoli tops with two chicken breasts laid over them, a delicate cream sauce poured over this, a dusting of Parmesan, and parsley. I've tried this and also with a base of spinach, but it wasn't the same. Hers was flavored by generosity and definitely by contrast with the hospital fare I had been living on.

MOM'S BIRDWATCHER'S CASSEROLE

Easy.

This is simply my daughter's name for cut-up chicken covered with a mix of 1 cup of raw rice, 1 package of onion-soup mix, 1 can of cream-of-mushroom soup diluted with sour cream, as many mushrooms as you like (or can afford), and some buttered bread crumbs sprinkled on top. Cover the casserole, and bake it for ¾ hour at 325°. Uncover for the last 10 minutes to crisp the bread-crumb topping.

WINE-AND-MUSHROOM CHICKEN

Fancier.

While you are lightly sautéing 1 cup of mushrooms, mix 3 tablespoons of flour with ½ cup of sour cream until the mixture is smooth. Add ½ teaspoon of salt, another ½ cup of sour cream, 1 can of undiluted cream-of-chicken soup, and ½ cup of Sauternes or Madeira. Blend the sauce well, then ladle it over 6 chicken breasts which have been folded over an herb dressing and sprinkled with Parmesan. Scatter chopped almonds and drained, chopped pimientos on top. Bake, covered, in a 325° oven until the chicken is tender (I don't know how long).

CHICKEN WINGS WITH PINEAPPLE SAUCE

Fanciest.

If chicken wings are too small for your taste, use broilers. You have to keep basting them. It makes a good barbecue, keeps the men occupied while the women toss salad and you heat the rolls you baked ahead.

Pineapple Sauce: Let 1 tablespoon each of minced garlic, minced onion, and water stand for 10 minutes with ½ teaspoon of powdered mustard to bring out the mustard flavor—no longer. Add 1 cup each of brown sugar and drained, crushed pineapple, ½ cup of cider vinegar, 2 tablespoons of soy sauce, a pinch each of cayenne and black pepper, 2 teaspoons of rosemary or thyme, ½ teaspoon of horseradish. Bring this to a boil, simmer it for 10 minutes, stirring it occasionally.

Brush the chicken wings with the sauce, and either barbecue or broil them slowly, basting constantly. If there is sauce left over, it will keep for another day.

NO-TEND CHICKEN

Cook together in a large pot, in an electric frying pan, or in a casserole 1 boned chicken breast per person, 2 sliced green peppers, 2 cans of stewed tomatoes, mushrooms, herbs, and seasoning until the chicken is done—½ to ¾ hour. Serve with rice, bulgur, or, more interestingly, sweet-and-sour millet.

Sweet-and-Sour Millet: Slowly drizzle 1 cup of millet, so that each grain gets wet, into 2 cups of boiling water, stock, or vegetable juice containing 1 clove of minced garlic and herbs. Simmer the ingredients, uncovered, for 15 minutes or until the liquid is absorbed. Then add 2 tablespoons each of oil, vinegar, and brown sugar, and simmer the millet 5 minutes longer. This is good by itself, as a replacement for rice, or added to soups, salads, and casseroles.

CHICKEN TETRAZZINI

This can also be made, depending on elegance and funds, with ham, corned beef, or shredded Spam. It is simply 1½ pounds of spaghetti or other pasta mixed with 3 cans of mushroom soup, 2 cups of milk or chicken broth, 2 cups of grated cheese, 2 teaspoons of parsley, 1 teaspoon of Worcestershire or soy sauce, heated in a casserole with the chicken or meat. Mushrooms, nutmeg, and a judicious amount of sherry will dress it up. It's useful.

CHICKEN CAPRI

Make this recipe a day or two ahead, and expand as needed. To 4 chicken breasts, add 2 cups of celery and 1 chopped, sautéed onion, ½ cup of broth, 1 can of mushroom soup, ½ cup or more of green-pepper and carrot slivers (for color), 1 can of chow-mein noodles, ½ cup of broken cashews. Before baking, sprinkle with some reserved noodles and more cashews.

CHICKEN PIE WITH CORN TOPPING

Anything can be done with chicken. In Bolivia, the following had several versions. This is the simplest, adapted to my American kitchen.

Place 1 cut-up chicken in a casserole, and top it with sliced, hard-boiled eggs, a handful of raisins, and some pitted olives. Spoon creamed corn mixed with a beaten egg, salt, and 1 tablespoon of sugar over this, and bake it until the chicken is tender. Sautéed onions, sliced tomatoes, a piece of butter, a pinch of cinnamon can be added (and would by me). Paprika shaken on top is a must.

POOR MAN'S BEEF STROGANOFF

Mary Durant, botanist-author, and her husband Michael Harwood, ornithologist-author, are responsible for the 622-page book *On the Road with John James Audubon* that I keep by my bed. You can't read a book that long steadily—at least I can't—but in the twenty minutes before I fall asleep, I enjoy delving into their travels, their camping and people adventures, their descriptions of our country as it was in John James and Lucy's day and as it is now. Our paths had crossed in the Dry Tortugas, at Great Gull Island, on Hawk Mountain, where Mike was gathering book material, so I was delighted to be staying with them after an Audubon program. Since the roads of their hilly town in western Connecticut glazed with ice after my arrival, my lecture had to be canceled and there was no hurry about dinner. Mary and Mike produced a potion to warm me and blank out my hours of driving. While Mary set rice to cook and dishes on a table angling off from the kitchen work space, I perched on a counter by the stove, admiring Mike as he concocted a Chinese dinner for us. It smelled *so* good, it looked so easy as he shook in this and added that—bamboo shoots and soy sauce, hot peppers and garlic, chunks of beef, oil heated to smoking, wine, peanuts, sesame oil. I picked up pencil and paper to record all this, but I had been too lulled by the warmth, our camaraderie, my drink to be able to make sense of my notes when I reached home. I do remember that at the end, everything was stir-fried and put over rice. The cooking was practically instantaneous.

"Easy and quick to make when you come in from birding," said Mike, flourishing his ladle. "Mary and I so often go off for the day, we specialize in meals that will cook by themselves, or in quick ones. I made this one after the Christmas Count this year—it takes no time at all. You *can* make it with chicken chunks you've cooked the day before if you want to, but that's a lot more trouble. This is just beef chunks, cut small, or ground beef if you are in a hurry, one-quarter pound per person. Add lots of onions, two cans of mushroom soup, a cup or more of stock (beef, chicken, or vegetable), two cups of sour cream, and dill. Cook this in a big pan on top of the stove, and, at the last minute, throw in as many frozen peas as you want, season, and dish over rice."

ALL-DAY CHICKEN

"Chicken," I said firmly, passing my plate for Chinese seconds. (My lecture is to be rescheduled; I plan to analyze those Chinese ingredients when I return. If it's Mike's week to cook— he and Mary alternate.) "We were talking about chicken. You said you had a wonderfully fragrant recipe. I'm trying to sort this cookbook into categories, you are tangling me up with Stroganoff."

He refilled my plate generously. "It's not my recipe," he said. "You'll have to credit Louise. She's a newspaper publisher in Goshen, New York, with an herb garden that supplies all her friends.

"I butter and salt a roasting chicken while Mary gets our breakfast. I sprinkle rosemary into the cavity, then fill this with onions—that's what keeps the chicken moist. Then I sprinkle the outside with more rosemary, drape the beast with bacon strips or salt pork, and set it, covered, to cook in a two hundred degree oven if we will be gone all day. Or I can bake it at normal temperature after I get home. Serve it with kugel. I trust you are putting rosemary into this book? It is marvelously fragrant."

"It also averts the evil eye and protects its plant neighbors from evil insects," added Mary the botanist. "It has a lot of historical values. Brides carried it as a symbol of fidelity. The blossoms are blue because the Virgin Mary threw her blue cloak over a bush of it on her flight to Egypt. In ancient days, students wore wreaths of it to refresh their memories during examinations. Thought to beautify hair, keep it from falling out, it is still used in hair tonics. It makes a good jelly, a fine herb tea, is excellent added to lemonade. It is in the mint family, so it goes well sprinkled on a roast of lamb. It's first-rate chopped into our turkey sandwiches, too."

That's enough on chicken.

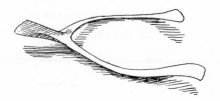

Rabbit

When I ran a birdbanding station in subtropical Florida, a neighbor kept Afghan hounds. If they got loose, they would slip down my lane to roll in the shallow pond I had had made for the birds I was studying. Herons came to fish in my pond; once, mysteriously, a white ibis, far from its habitat, folded its black-tipped wings, reconnoitered, sampled the small mosquito fish, and then walked out into the lane and away, obviously disappointed. Robins, blackbirds, and songbirds disported themselves in the reeds about the pond, splittering and splattering, drinking, leaving their prints in the soft sand at the edge among those of the raccoon and possum that visited at night. My pond's chorus of toads and frogs in spring could be heard for half a mile. (I pointed out to complaining insomniacs that their dogs' barking kept *me* awake.)

Because the Afghans often became tangled in my bird mist nets, I came to know well their owners and the young sons who were supposed to keep them at home. To placate me, the boys would bring fat young rabbits they raised for their family table—skinned (I immediately made that part of the deal). Although my well-used *Joy of Cooking* gives explicit directions for skinning rabbits (and squirrels), my tolerance went only so far.

"How do I cook this critter?" I asked them the first time they arrived with their gift, nervously apologetic, hounds straining on ropes. Over the telephone, their mother came to my rescue. Stewed, fried, or roasted, she taught me. Fried was quickest. It was an expensive dish (nets are expensive and Afghans clumsy). I learned to enjoy the rabbits, and the occasional guinea fowl another neighbor provided (also dressed) in exchange for the opportunity of photographing the tanagers and anis, painted and indigo buntings I would hold in my hand for him.

FRIED RABBIT

Treat it like chicken—cut it into serving pieces. Be sure it is young, and marinate it overnight in red wine. Shake it in a paper bag with flour, salt, and herbs, then cook it in fairly deep fat for about 25 minutes or more. (If you are taking birds out of a net in the back forty—which I always was doing at dusk—you can't keep an eye on the clock.)

ROAST RABBIT

It should be mature. Again, treat it like chicken. Marinate it for a day or more in 2 cups of wine. I rub it with oil and herbs and *lots* of garlic, and baste it as often as I can. These animals are practically impossible to stuff, but you can shove herbs and garlic inside. Cook it long and slowly, and eat it with rice.

RABBIT BRAISED

If you want to forget a cooking rabbit while you work, you can braise it, though you do have to check to make sure the liquid—½ cup each of water and wine, plus 1 tablespoon of vinegar for every 2 pounds of meat—doesn't boil dry. Brown your critter in oil, then steam it on a rack over very low heat for at least 2½ hours. Figure out your own seasoning—salt, pepper, herbs, but always garlic. I'm not sure rabbit isn't an acquired taste for people brought up on beef, but I learned to like it.

HUNTER'S RABBIT STEW

This is more trouble.

Cut the rabbit into serving pieces, and marinate it for a few hours or overnight. Render small chunks of salt pork, about ¼ pound of this. When most of the fat is out, slice in an onion and, if you have any, mushrooms, and sauté these, then remove them and the pork. Dredge the rabbit pieces with flour and herbs, sauté them with garlic in the salt-pork fat, add as much vegetable or chicken stock or dry wine or tomato juice or canned tomatoes as seems reasonable, and simmer all this with bay leaves for at least 1 hour. Toward the end, put back the onion, mushrooms, and salt pork you have reserved, add cut-up celery, and cook the stew until the celery is done—about 15 minutes. Sprinkle with chopped parsley for color (and health).

Meats

CHILI RABBIT

I really wowed a group with this one night.

Again, brown marinated rabbit pieces with garlic. Put them in a bean pot with 1 can of stock or chicken broth, 1 small can of tomato paste, 1 spoonful of chili powder. The rabbit should simmer for 2 hours. Then add 1 1-pound can of kidney beans. You can increase these ingredients, depending on how much rabbit you have, how many you are feeding.

(When I told my guests what they were eating, it was almost as much fun as the night I served a casserole made from my Rhode Island Red rooster. He had savaged me to the point where I had to ax him if I was to survive his attacks as I watered his ladies and collected their eggs. He was a tough bird. I cooked him several ways for a week. Finally, after being soaked in wine for a full day and night, he became edible in a casserole, well concealed among mushrooms and vegetables. Delicious, although maybe, as I rubbed my scars and Band-aids, my opinion was biased.)

WINGED RABBIT

You have to *think,* though. On Cape Cod one day, to introduce northern friends to rabbit, I bought a frozen one. The directions on the package said to use honey in the marinade. I didn't *think.* When I came to clean my electric frying pan, several packs of S.O.S later I decided it would be easier to buy a new one—the honey was permanently fused in. Oh, well— I really needed a new pan anyway. This one had seen heavy service, was overdue for replacement. It had been given to me by Ian Nisbet one summer when I house-mothered his orni-

thological research crew, studying tern colonies on Cape Cod. While it was a sentimental wrench to send it to the Salvation Army, I balanced this with my story to subsequent guests of the woman who had returned the piece of rabbit I had put on her plate, saying she preferred a drumstick to a wing. Wings on a rabbit?

Guinea Fowl

Guineas are dry. You must rub them well with oil and roast them under a thin covering of salt-pork strips, basting frequently. You hope you get a young one, and cook it the way you would a chicken—in a 350° oven. Or you can steam it on a rack like rabbit, over ½ cup each of wine and water, and 1 tablespoon of vinegar, for a couple of hours if you don't want the bother of basting. I really prefer my guinea hens in trees, setting up their loud alarm rackets at any intruder to their domain. But a gift is a gift (particularly if you are hungry and broke, as, at the time, I was).

Goose

I've never cooked a Canada goose. They are plentiful on my salt pond on Cape Cod. They used to fly in hundreds over Dottie Mendinhall's birdbanding station on the Chesapeake, their wings beating low and loudly over our heads, their calls reaching deep into my pedestrian spirit. They have skeined my skies in too many happy places, have been too much a symbol of wild beauty for me to be able to truss and stuff one. The nearest I ever got was when Joe Hickey came to call with one that had been skinned, greased, and stuffed in his suitcase so that he might take it to his daughter for Thanksgiving.

Dove

LITTLE DOVES

In Australia, people birdwatch and get hungry, too. A hostess one night served us Little Doves.

She had separated cabbage leaves, set them in cold water for 5 minutes, then drained them and wrapped them neatly about a big spoonful of mix. This was made from 1½ pounds of seasoned lean ground beef (for 6 of us), 2 cups of cooked rice, 1 cup of catsup, and enough broth to moisten. Not too moist. She covered the bottom of a baking dish with 1 inch of broth or rice water, set the rolled up Little Doves in this, dotted them with butter, and baked them, covered, for 1 hour at 300°. Then she added more sauce, or broth and catsup, as needed, and baked the dish for another hour. This can be cooked the day before and reheated. Ten minutes before serving, she instructed, ½ pint of cream is added, and the doves finish cooking, uncovered. (She knew I was, at the time, on the National Audubon Society's Board, so I wondered if she had substituted beef for the ample supply of doves available about their yard, but thought it mannerly not to ask. *I* would use dove breasts for this; they'd be better than ground beef! A better conversation piece, too.)

If you are a Bird Lady like me, you are brought birds that have crashed against windows, that the cat has brought in, or that have been found flapping by a golf course or a sprayed agricultural field. If I live where one is near enough, I take them to a rehabilitation center that I think does good work, or tend to them in my own aviary. They are mostly dead or dying. Their skins are valuable for study specimens in museums or nature centers. Their bodies—miniature as some may be once I have peeled the skin off, cleaned the skulls, the legs, and the wings—I eye their bodies thoughtfully. They could go into my compost heap, where a nocturnal animal would dig them up, enjoy them, or—well, I *am* always careful to inquire where and how the bird has been found. Doves are meaty and delicious; but if they come from territory sprayed with pesticides (that's why they have been found dying), I think it better that a raccoon eat them instead of me. There are too many raccoons these days; we have killed off the larger animals that predated them. But if it is a duck, a quail, a grosbeak, a cedar waxwing . . . Some are tough, some tender—a change on my dinner plate from chicken and hamburger. The small ones frizzle up very fast in a bit of butter. The larger ones need to be wrapped in bacon.

Oddments (Good for Lunches Also)

TAMALE PIE

Blonde, lovely Ann lives in what was once a remote California canyon. She is a hummingbird watcher. Tied by emphysema to a 50-foot cord and an oxygen tank, she has had syrup feeders hung at her windows, enjoying the freedom of the colored mites that speed and dart to them, dipping their wings, we feel, in recognition of her. She taught me how to make this Tamale Pie. It allows for many variations. She uses ground beef or ham chunks or sausage, vegetables being added ad lib (depending on how many people are coming over), onions and garlic, green peppers, hot peppers, drained tomatoes or undiluted tomato soup, ½ cup of red kidney beans, 1 can or frozen package of whole-kernel corn, 1 full cup of extra-sharp grated cheese, chili powder (1 tablespoon or 1 teaspoon, according to the geographical background of her guests), a good dash of Tabasco (ditto), 1 teaspoon of cumin, salt, and halved black olives. Three large tamales cut in pieces or Fritos can be used as a topping. She lets this mellow overnight. For a really hearty dish, she spreads corn-bread mix very thinly on this just before baking, bakes the pie in a medium oven until the corn bread is done.

For vegetarians, I substitute lima beans and more red kidney beans for the meat, add carrot slivers, mushrooms if I have any.

SAUSAGE CRISPS

Stir 2 cups of milk into ⅔ cup of flour until the mixture is smooth. Add 3 beaten eggs and 1 teaspoon of salt. Beat the batter well, and spread it over a thin layer of sausage meat. Bake in a hot oven until it is brown. "This is very rich, and very good on a cold day," wrote Mrs. E. A. Hardy in a cookbook "Revised and Enlarged by the Barnstable Village Improvement Society in 1911." "Just as good now as then," says her great-granddaughter, serving it to us for lunch.

SCRAPPLE

At the small market on the Chesapeake where we bought crabmeat, I could get a scrapple such as I have never tasted before or since. We ate it, sliced thin and fried, at Dottie Mendinhall's birdbanding station every day for breakfast, if I could arrange this. It came in 2-pound bricks. I would carry some to Washington when I left, though my urban diplomatic friends, I soon learned, preferred omelets and croissants, not being used to Birders' Breakfasts. One year I even froze some to take to south Florida with me, keeping the bricks iced en route, stashing them in my hosts' freezers. The rules I found for making scrapple all called for pigs' feet or hogs' heads or similarly unattractive internal ingredients. Lacking these, what I managed was unsatisfactory.

EVELYN'S SCRAPPLE

I remembered a farm woman in Pennsylvania who had been disappointed one fall when I had stopped through and wouldn't stay to help her butcher her hogs. Maybe I should have—her scrapple was marvelous. It came for breakfast in big sheets, as taken for granted as toast or eggs. What a change from doughnuts or croissants! I wrote, asking for her recipe. No answer. So I telephoned. She apologized, said it was a problem in mathematics, but if I wanted to work it out—

Starts with a 48-gallon kettle, 3 pigs, and 1 steer, using bones, liver, kidneys, and other interior organs. Put in water to cover. When the meat falls off the bone with cooking, remove the bones, grind the meat, and return the meat to the kettle with 2 pounds of coriander. (Did you know that coriander can be bought by the *pound?*) Add lots of salt, bring the liquid to a boil. When the broth boils, add slowly, stirring—it must never lump—4 pounds of corn meal (a special kind, I think—roasted. Does corn meal come roasted? Toasted?). Her dogs were barking; I couldn't hear her clearly. Then she stirs in 10 pounds of buckwheat flour, 10 pounds of whole-wheat flour, 4 pounds of pastry flour, and all-purpose flour until the scrapple "leaves the kettle" (that's a culinary term for getting stiff enough not to adhere to the sides of the pot). She puts what has now resulted in 230 to 265 pounds of scrapple into pans, cools it, slices it, and puts it in her freezer, which is larger than mine. Some people, she says, use rosemary, but she doesn't

like it. Our telephone connection was poor, the dogs inter-
fered, I don't guarantee all these measurements. But if you
have a 48-gallon kettle, 3 pigs, 1 steer, and a large freezer
. . . She urged me, if I could work out the proportions, to try
stirring some up on my stove. Only don't forget the bones,
she said, the livers, the kidneys . . . Thanks, Evelyn.

Vegetarian

It is time we took notice of vegetarians. There are more and more of them, they need to be fed, too, I want to keep them as my friends. Only time will tell if they are healthier than meat eaters. The nonvegetarians can utilize the following recipes by adding chunks or bits of cooked ham, lamb, beef.

I would add goat, too, if I could get any. Lydia Hale breeds registered pygmy goats. I called her to see if she might have a specialty from her kitchen, which is blanketed with prize-winning ribbons. Her father, Joe Lund, was an ardent birder, a founder of the Manomet Bird Observatory, a friend of ours since Harvard days. Liddy was horrified at the suggestion that she might *eat* one of the denizens of her immaculate barn, didn't even know how to go about cooking one.

MEXICAN CASSEROLE

There are innumerable versions to offer a vegetarian. You have to like corn, you have to like hot peppers, garlic, beans of many sorts, and accept whatever cheeses are available. Mexicans use tortillas and tamales in casseroles the way we do rice and pasta. Often these are cut into strips with a sauce of sautéed onions, tomatoes, garlic added to vegetable water or broth and layered over whatever vegetables are available—those starchy root ones I see in Mexican markets, knobby, and don't know their names or uses. Here we could use beans, limas, carrots, peas, olives. When the ingredients are heated through, spread grated cheese over the top, and run the dish under the broiler.

GARBANZOS CON CEBOLLA

Garbanzos are chickpeas, good in cold salads, hot soups, casserole, on toothpicks dipped in cocktail sauces.

For this dish, soak the dried peas overnight, then simmer them with garlic, bay leaf, and seasoning for 1½ more hours. And *lots* of onions that have been sautéed or stewed and as much tomato, canned or fresh, as you want. You can do this ahead and reheat the dish. As above, tortillas, tamales, or tacos can be added. Meat, for those who want it—chunks of cooked ham, lamb, beef, pork, or goat. Goat is especially good (the Mexicans must have a special way of cooking it). Make a casserole for each diet.

CHURCH SUPPER FOR LOTS

Plain, hearty, rather bland.

Two boxes of noodles—1 thin, 1 wide—2 large cans of tomatoes, 2 teaspoons of brown sugar, 2 teaspoons of Worcestershire sauce, seasoning, 1 or 2 large onions and green pepper, sliced. Set these in a large casserole, top them with grated cheese, and bake slowly for 2 hours. More cheese, incorporated, would make the dish more nourishing and tastier.

GINNY'S NOODLES

These are sturdier.

To 1 package of noodles or other cooked pasta, she adds 8 ounces or more of cottage cheese thinned with milk, and cubed Cheddar. This is topped with bread crumbs, yellow cheese for color, and is dotted with butter for a crusty top. If the casserole gets too dry, she adds more milk. To this base, she adds as she wishes mushrooms, onions, peppers (green or hot), tomato sauce, and, for nonvegetarians, seafood or meat.

DOG SUPPER

This was served to us in Vermont at a Church Supper. Delicious. The women looked down their noses at me when I asked for measurements. A Vermonter obviously knows instinctively how to combine summer squash with onions, mushrooms, and cheese in a casserole. They didn't even explain the name. Myself, I'd sauté the onion before adding it and judge the other proportions by how many people I was feeding. This may be the same recipe, more or less, that I give under "Pumpkin" (page 119).

CHEESE WOODCHUCK

From Maine. I'd like to know why this name, too!

Sauté a small onion; add ⅔ cup of milk, 2 cups of whole-kernel corn, ½ pound of diced cheese, a dash of Worcestershire sauce, and seasoning. Heat the ingredients until the cheese is melted, add 2 beaten eggs, and cook gently 2 to 3 minutes longer. Safer to cook it in a double boiler while the fishermen shuck their wet clothes.

DEREK'S RICE

Derek the Driver has trouble walking, so he birds by telescope from his car window. When our day is over, he has been sitting too long. He puts on an apron and heads for the kitchen—any kitchen. His specialty is to toss sautéed onion, broccoli, parsley, and Romano into hot rice (preferably brown) during the last minutes of its cooking.

With this for meat eaters, he serves big center slices of ham spread with good mustard, brown sugar, apples sliced with the skin still on, and pineapple chunks, if a can is handy. These bake slowly while the rice cooks and he prepares the broccoli.

Since he likes color, he often cooks young carrots until they are just tender, cuts them in half, dips them in warmed honey, then layers them in a generously buttered baking dish with seasoning and an equally generous topping of grated Swiss cheese. These bake in the oven with the ham slices.

SWEET-AND-SOUR CARROTS

Sometimes he arrives with this prepared casserole.

Boil 2 pounds of carrot coins until they are barely tender. Add 1 onion and 1 green pepper, chopped; spread half of these in a casserole, cover with sauce (see below), and repeat the layering process. Refrigerate the dish at least overnight.

Sauce: Combine ¼ cup of cider vinegar, ½ cup of salad oil, 1 teaspoon of soy sauce, 1 teaspoon of dry mustard, salt, and pepper. Heat the sauce slowly (with or without those ham slices).

DEVILED CARROTS .

Derek also puts in a pan strips of carrots, ¼ cup of butter, a sprinkling of salt, and cooks them, tightly covered, until the carrots are tender. (Don't let them burn.) He then combines 2 teaspoons of honey, ½ teaspoon of dry mustard, freshly ground pepper, and ¼ teaspoon of salt, and adds this to the carrots, stirring and turning to coat the strips evenly. These are simmered, covered, a few minutes longer and served at once.

BAKED CARROTS

Combine 4 sliced carrots with 2 sliced apples (peel the apples, unless you are lazy). Drizzle over these 2 tablespoons of maple syrup or molasses, 2 tablespoons of butter, and 2 tablespoons of brown sugar, and bake for 30 minutes more or less until the carrots are tender.

COOKED CARROT SALAD

We seem to be specializing in carrots. They are recommended for Owlers' night vision. The following is *not* a soup. Good on a hot day.

Slice and cook 2 pounds of carrots. Cool them, and cover them with 1 slice of green pepper, 1 large red onion sliced in rings, 1 can of tomato soup. Pour over this a marinade of ½ cup of salad oil, ¾ cup of vinegar, ½ cup of sugar, 1 teaspoon each of soy sauce and dry mustard, salt, and pepper. Chill the salad thoroughly.

RICE PILAF

Birders *do* eat other vegetables. The vegetables can be stir-fried, boiled, stewed, raw; in combination or singly. Writing all this about just carrots has tired me out, so I'll let you hunt up recipes on your own. I do particularly, though, like to make rice pilaf.

Sauté 1 large onion, add 2 cups of rice pilaf or just ordinary bulgur, sauté the ingredients for 5 minutes. Then add 2 cups of beef bouillon, salt, ⅓ cup of raisins. Bring this to a boil, remove the pilaf from the heat, let it stand for 5 minutes, stir in ¾ cup of slice almonds and a handful of chopped parsley. Eat the pilaf hot or cold.

OKRA

Maybe okra is a southern dish. It's gummy; I have trouble selling it to my northern friends. A northerner also, I tried it first because it was such a ridiculous looking vegetable, growing like rows of sticks in the Florida fields. Then I discovered how useful it was in soups and stews and casseroles, in fritatas, how delicious just plain. Since it's hard to find in northern stores, I buy (frozen) all I can when I find it. If you like it, let me know and come for lunch.

(1) It can be sliced and sautéed with bread crumbs and parsley. First boil the pods for about 3 minutes. Then sauté the okra with ½ cup of corn meal added to the butter—that's really southern.

(2) It's good sautéed (after boiling) with onion, green pepper, a pinch of oregano or basil, and, again, parsley.

(3) For a full luncheon dish, you can add 1 cup of corn and 2 or 3 tomatoes to preparation number 2, plus a little chopped celery and the herbs.

I like it a lot added to soups and stews; it thickens as well as flavors.

BRAISED CELERY

Only I don't think "braised" is the proper word. I make it because it is easy, it uses up those big outer stalks that are otherwise only good for soup or tuna salad, and I *like* it.

Chop the outer stalks of a bunch of celery, and stew them in 1 cup of vegetable stock or water with a beef-bouillon cube added. Stew them slowly—for as long as you wish (the longer, the better). Any leftovers, and definitely the leftover liquid, get added to soup. I am always being asked how I make my soups. I am embarrassed to tell. Except for cauliflower, cabbage, and Brussels sprouts, liquid left from almost anything goes into my "soup saver." It upsets me to see people pour off vegetable stock, discard chicken bones. When you have lived on islands or mountains far from civilization, you have learned to make do and find unexpected richness and interest in the necessary experiments. Remember those chicken feet on page 18, or would you rather not contemplate them?

A SUCCULENCE OF MUSHROOMS

A sauce for whatever.

To 1 cup of sour cream, mix 1 tablespoon of flour, a little grated onion, salt, paprika. You can add any gravy (or celery stock) to this to extend it, if needed. Pour over 1 pound of sautéed mushroom.

Squash and Pumpkin

Cookbooks are full of squash recipes. Each year, vegetable bins at markets display new and more colorful kinds. I've experimented because now that I no longer have young children to slice eyes and tooth-filled mouths into pumpkins at Halloween, I pile varicolored squash for decoration at my door and later bring them in, one by one, to cook.

ACORN SQUASH AND APPLE

My favorite recipe, I think, because it is so quick and easy—a one-dish meal.

Halve some acorn squash, and remove the fibers and seeds (which birds and squirrels will appreciate). Fill the hollows with chopped apple, a spoonful of brown sugar, and top this with sausage meat (see the recipe, below). Cover with foil, put in the oven, and forget them. They cook in about 45 minutes, longer with lower heat if you want to go out, and will keep—the timing depends on my convenience and that of the visitors in my living room. (I was taught this recipe by a man who hates to get his hands greasy, so skips the cookbook admonition of rubbing the squash, inside and out, with butter.)

For vegetarians, omit the sausage, add more apple, and top with chutney.

Miss Emily's Pork Sausage: That fastidious man had a southern wife, Miss Emily, who liked to make her own sausage. You had to be careful—she put plenty of red hot pepper in it.

Have your butcher grind 2 pounds of lean fresh pork. Add 1 tablespoon each of salt and black pepper, 2 teaspoons of sage, 2 finely chopped hot-pepper pods. (Pepper pods come in different sizes and strengths—you need to adjust your tongue to them. Miss Emily liked them big and dry.)

ACORN SQUASH (ADDENDUM)

Once you have cooked the halves (the easiest way is to cut them, then steam them until they are soft), they can be stuffed with creamed chicken, chipped beef with mushrooms, ham and beans, corn, or just a cooked vegetable mix, then baked in a slow oven until you are ready.

Squash and pumpkins keep well frozen. Use them, mashed with a fork or puréed, for soups, casserole, pumpkin bread, pie. They are inexpensive, often free if you bring one home from a hostess's decorative, passé Halloween or Thanksgiving arrangement.

"What will you do with them?" a friend asked me curiously the other night, offering me a second one from her doorstep, then a third—a big one—watching me feel them to be sure they weren't soft. I told her. "But doesn't that take a lot of time?"

Well, everything takes time. You either pay someone else for theirs or use your own—it's a choice. I tried doing part-time work for a while. That meant acquiring suitable clothes, paying babysitters, imposing on my friends to bring my children home from school, buying prepared and, therefore, expensive goods at market. I didn't stick with this long enough to work up to a managerial position—I was running a typewriter and a telephone. I decided that the financial recompense wasn't worth it, that if I were going to work that hard I'd rather be at home, working creatively for my family. My compost heap nourished my garden, and so my family and friends. We had flowers for our spirit, home-grown tomatoes, a quince tree for jams; my market bills were halved. I had time for a husband, children, friends, and occasional free-lance work. I didn't feel put-upon, exploited. I wasn't being harassed by people whose job was to get as much work as possible out of me (I suspect my family did that, but it was different). I didn't have to stand on aching feet, as did some of the women and men who came to our office for help.

I grant that the world has changed. I grant that staying home with small children can be boring, even stultifying— but only if you let it. In each of us, there is a creative part to nourish. It's a question of values, of where you want to put your time. Only you can decide. I was lucky; I had a man to bring home a paycheck. I worked at keeping him, at loving him.

I see our culture—waiting in airports, driving on crowded highways as I must. I watch tourists mill idly about the gift shops of resort towns, families climbing into campers and vans that hurry from one state park to another—people Going Somewhere, Anywhere, in order to avoid looking at their lives, to avoid asking themselves what they really want out of their time. If we each thought we had only a year remaining to us, how would we spend it? Sitting in traffic jams? Gandering at Mt. Rushmore? Climbing lighthouse stairs or the moss-grown steps of some ancient temple just to say we had done this? Trying not to weep in a divorce lawyer's office? We each have different needs, satisfactions; it's a matter of deciding. Of course, often we make make wrong decisions. I didn't approve of my mother's. I doubt my daughter approves of mine. I tolerate hers. It's what makes lives so complex and interesting.

This is supposed to be a cookbook.

PUMPKIN CASSEROLE

A German countrywoman fed me this.

Mix 6 cups of mashed pumpkin with 3 cups of cut-up ham, 1½ cups of thick cream sauce, and 1½ cups of sharp Cheddar. Put half of the mixture in an oiled casserole, cover it with 2 or 3 sliced, hard-boiled eggs, add the rest, top it with crumbled crackers (or Fritos; sesame seeds would be my change). Sprinkle on more grated cheese, dot with butter, bake for 30 minutes. And—except for the ham—there you have a Vermont Dog Supper!

I would add chopped green and red peppers to this, perhaps a little onion, but Hulda cooked before these were common staples.

BROCCOLI AND SQUASH CASSEROLE

Squash comes in such sizes and shapes, you pick what appeals to you for however many you plan to feed. A butternut (big) or its equivalent will probably feed 6. If there is too much, you can make a good soup from the overage.

Steam your squash (or pumpkin) in 1 cup of water until soft enough to peel, remove the seeds and fiber, cut into bite-sized pieces. Set these in a casserole with 2 tablespoons of margarine and ½ cup of vegetable stock or water left from the steaming. Bake this, covered, for 15 minutes. Add broccoli flowerets (saving the big stems for soup—see below) and 1 cup of chicken broth or 1 cup of water with 2 bouillon cubes. Bake again until the broccoli is tender but still crisp; then drizzle 1 teaspoon of ground cardamom that has been stirred into 4 tablespoons of butter melted with the juice of ½ lemon. (My shop didn't have ground cardamom, just pods, so I used these. Not the same result!)

If there are leftovers, cook your big broccoli stems (peeled) the next day, and put them in a blender. Season this, add sour cream, rinse out your blender with as much milk or cream as the soup needs, and, presto, here are two meals for the price of one. Scatter the squash seeds for your birds. (I tried toasting pumpkin seeds once, but no one seemed to enjoy them. So now I toss them out for wildlife. Someone eats them; they disappear.)

Beans

Beans have nourished man through history. There are innumerable kinds, cooked in innumerable ways. In our culture, mostly after boiling them until tender, we bake them long and slowly with onions, garlic, tomatoes, sweet or hot peppers, spices, molasses, salt pork, ham, sausage. They can be baked with beer, with fruit—apples, pineapple, prunes, wine, apricots, raisins—cooked in an oven, in a hole in the ground. The following are recipes that I use most often. Remember that 1 cup of dried beans will yield 2 to 2½ cups when cooked.

BAKED BEANS

Red kidney beans are what most people think of as baked beans.

To 1 cup of dried beans, cooked (the package or any cookbook will tell you how) and drained, add, without much attention to the measurements, ½ cup of chopped onion, 2 minced garlic cloves, and 1 cup of tomato relish (that is, my own mixture of onions, peppers, celery—but chili sauce or catsup or tomato sauce plus a chopped sweet or hot pepper is acceptable). To this add a dash of vinegar, ½ cup of molasses (that's important), ½ cup of tomato juice or beer, 1 tablespoon of soy sauce, about ½ cup of tomatoes. If I use salt pork (⅓ pound), I render most of the fat out of it first. Since this takes time, I am more apt to substitute small pieces of sausage or chopped ham. All of this cooks in a bean pot—a real bean pot, clay, heavy, its cover removed at the end. Beans can cook all day, even overnight for those 4 A.M. Owlers. If they look dry (the beans—the Owlers will definitely look dry at that hour), add more beer or tomato juice or the water that the beans cooked in.

FRIJOLES NEGROS (BLACK BEANS)

From New Mexico.

Cook 1 pound of dried black beans in ample water according to package directions, adding ½ each of a chopped green pepper and chopped onion, 2 crushed garlic cloves, 1 teaspoon of salt, 3 bay leaves, oregano, and 1 tablespoon of olive oil. When the beans are soft (in about 2 hours) and the water cooked down, sauté the other ½ pepper and onion with 2 more crushed garlic cloves in a heavy skillet with a ladle full of the beans. Then add this to the beans, and continue cooking until they are thickened but not burned (that's the trick). Just before serving them over rice, add 1 tablespoon (or more) of sherry or rum and 1 tablespoon of sugar. White rice is more pleasing to the eye, brown more nutritious. Any leftovers can be refried (see below).

FRIJOLES REFRITOS (REFRIED BEANS)

All you do for this is mash up your beans, add a little cheese (not Roquefort!), and fry them like a pancake in hot oil. They are very good with sausage patties and apples. If you are a vegetarian, eat them with tomato juice and an apple-and-walnut salad.

BEAN COCKTAIL DIP

If there are Refried Beans left over, don't toss them out.

This was fed me in California at a wine-and-cheese book signing, en route to a meeting of the Santa Clara Audubon Society, where we topped off with coffee and Oreos. It was a solid dish, attractive to look at, and no trouble at all to make, said Lynn Tennefosse, in charge of it and me.

Gently refry the beans with Cheddar (and a lump of butter to keep the beans from solidifying) and salsa, the amounts depending upon the amount of beans. Put these in a shallow decorative bowl, and cover them thickly with chopped tomatoes and avocados. Set out crackers strong enough not to break (which tortilla chips will).

If any of *this* is left over, it makes good sandwiches, as I found out at daybreak the next morning, when I was picked up to go to Dick Mewalt's banding station.

Potatoes

Potatoes can be cooked in as many ways as beans. Buy thin-skinned ones, and eat the skins (that's where their nutrition is highest). Study their history, and be impressed. If there isn't time to bake them (which is, of course, the easiest cooking method—be sure to scrub the skins and eat those, too—restaurants *charge* for potato skins!), boil them, and serve them with butter and parsley. Or mash them. All that butter may not be good for you and you can train yourself to do without, but it makes a fine dish. If you have more time, try the following.

POTATOES OF THE HOUSE

Cube 6 boiled potatoes (you boiled them while you were waiting for the tide, before you went to see what birds had blown in on last night's storm). Sauté 2 sliced onions; add 2 cups of stewed tomatoes (or 4 fresh ones, cut up), 1 teaspoon of salt, ½ teaspoon each of basil and paprika, and the potatoes; bake this at 350° in a casserole, and sprinkle with parsley. (*Always* sprinkle potatoes with parsley.)

POTATO KUGEL

This recipe comes from a woman in Wisconsin who joined our birdbanding group on Nantucket one week. She had never heard the word *diet,* preferred cooking to birdwatching, kept us all happy. I think I have this odd dish correctly—it allows for variations. It can be served hot or cold, but if you plan to use it cold, *do not add the yogurt.*

Boil 6 potatoes with 2 or 3 carrots, 1 big onion, 1 garlic clove. Drain (and save the liquid for soup another day). Add 2 beaten eggs, 3 tablespoons of oil, 2 teaspoons of salt, ¼ cup of bread crumbs, ¾ cup of dry milk. Bake this for 40 to 60 minutes, depending on the depth of your pan. It will be like a cake, with its edges brown. Add quickly either ½ to 1 cup of grated cheese, or 2 cups of yogurt and ⅓ cup of cheese. Return the pan to the oven for 5 minutes to melt this topping.

FISK POTATOES FOR LUNCH

When I have potatoes left over, sometimes I put them into vegetable soup, sometimes I make cream-of-potato soup with careful seasoning—a little finely chopped celery and onion, a dash of curry, chicken broth, sour cream (if I have any) or milk (if I am having trouble zipping my jeans). But mostly I am apt to fry them with lots of onion and as much sweet or hot pepper and celery as pleases me at the moment. If I need to make a whole meal of these, I add leftover sausage or meat or bacon. These are white potatoes. With sweet potatoes, I mash and brown them in butter, though it doesn't hurt to mix in a little orange or crushed pineapple. You don't have to eat sandwiches every noon.

CANDIED SWEET POTATOES

Boil and peel 6 sweet potatoes, or use 3 packages of frozen ones, if you are lazy. Slice them the long way; put them in a shallow buttered pan, and pour over them ½ to 1 cup of brown sugar melted in 1 tablespoon of butter for each potato. Add 2 or 3 spoonfuls of fresh orange juice (or frozen orange juice), grated orange rind, and 2 or 3 pieces of candied ginger cut fine. This is so good as is that I hesitate to add any crushed pineapple to it, but some do. Bake the potatoes for about 20 minutes at 400°, less if the top gets too brown (although it is good crusty). It can be baked covered, too. There's a lot of leeway. (Once I had a recipe that used 2 beaten eggs, but it was lost or stolen. I guess that would be Sweet-Potato and Orange Puff—it had some real orange in it, too.)

The Christmas Count

The Annual Audubon Christmas Count began in 1900 as a way to enjoy birds in the field other than with a gun. Eighty-six competitive years later, it has resulted in—I quote Susan Drennan, editor of the Society's *American Birds*—"the most extensive, longest-term, comprehensive data set in American ornithology. In 1985, 41,377 observers counted 108,948,275 birds in 1478 Count Circles" from Alaska to the West Indies, from Maine to Central America. The teams sallied forth in temperatures that ranged in 1985 from 92° in Panama to −45°

in Alberta, Canada, set standards that influence birdwatching all through the year. For many of its practitioners, birding is a highly competitive sport, demanding unflagging stamina from 4:00 A.M., when a team may set out to flush nocturnal species, to the final hours of dusk, when they gather in hospitable homes to tally, telephone about the country for rival scores, and *eat*. The social hours, the stops for quick refreshment are important, excited, happy parts of an exhausting day.

I don't know what a team eats for breakfast in Panama or Costa Rica. But in the blustery winds and cold of a Count in the North, a hostess can't go wrong with a large pot of baked beans and molasses that has simmered overnight in a slow oven, available to the earliest risers and to those who come stamping in later to warm their bones and bellies. Codfish cakes and sausage often go with this, toasted corn bread (with beach-plum jelly, if you live on Cape Cod or the neighboring islands).

In the South, Black-eyed Peas bring you at New Year's good fortune, so these show up on Count menus. They can be cooked the same way as are northern red kidney beans—with molasses, onion, and pork. The traditional Soul Food of the South is rice, pork, and beans of some type. So when you stop mid-morning to consolidate cars, change drivers, warm cold hands with pots of hot coffee, it is near enough to New Year's to get, in the South, the traditional Christmas-week Black-eyed Rabbit. I told you about this. It's simple fare that can simmer in a chafing dish. If I describe it again, I'll get an editorial frown. So turn back to page 63.

ENGLISH MONKEY

This dish is similar minus the lucky peas. You can whip it up when you see cars driving in, while their occupants mill about under the mistletoe.

In a hot, heavy skillet, heat 1 cup each of dry bread crumbs, grated cheese, and milk with 1 teaspoon of prepared mustard. Stir until the cheese melts (about 3 minutes) and the ingredients are blended. Then spoon the sauce over toast or English muffins. This can be made in any proportions or in successive relays; but it will be only as good as your cheese, so use the best. Serve it with beer, sherry, coffee, or Irish coffee, depending upon your geographical location and your guests. It can be accompanied by baked apples (see below).

BAKED APPLES

These may have the standard filling of brown sugar, cinnamon and nuts or, for the holiday, of mincemeat. Pour over the apples a syrup made of 1 cup of sugar, 2 tablespoons of butter, and ⅓ cup of water; cook them until they are soft. They can be kept warm for the North, cold for the South.

CORN CHOWDER I

When you stop at noon, you have no leisure—the pressure is on. This applies equally to Birdathons and Big Days. Your time is more than half gone, your list not yet adequate. This is when hearty soups with vegetables, rice, lentils, beans, barley, millet are really needed. And chowders.

This one of Ginger's is special. It has traveled in kettles many miles about Connecticut for the sustenance of hawk watchers, eagle searchers, more earthbound Counters who are finding mostly jays and juncos, and for far-flung Christmas teams.

The basic recipe—for heaven's sake, at least double it—is

¼ pound or more of bacon partially cooked and the grease poured off. To this add in whatever proportions you want chopped onion, diced potatoes, and green peppers, sautéing these a bit in the pan, which will still be greasy. Add sliced carrots and parsley. Drain 2 or more cans of corn; blend 2 to 4 heaping tablespoons of flour with the liquid, and add this to the pan. Simmer all this—Ginger means *simmer*—then put the corn in, whatever seasoning you want, a suitable quantity of milk, heat, and pour into your kettle. If the kettle isn't full, make some more—it will be appreciatively eaten, with cheese and any variety of breads. A small jar of pimientos, chopped, and a sprinkling of parsley add Christmas color.

CORN CHOWDER II

A different Corn Chowder, more ladylike, was eaten by three of us—two avid birdwatchers and an avid botanist—at Longwood Gardens in Delaware one fall day, when we were temporarily resting our feet. We tried to analyze it. Part of the fun of eating is deciding what is in a dish, going home to replicate it. If you don't succeed, at least you come up with something interesting.

Corn, of course, we decided—chopped very small but not puréed. Potatoes chopped very small, not too many. Onion, not much. Bits of celery, flicks of red and green pepper, chunks of chicken breast, and thyme. A cream sauce that must have been chicken broth thinned with half-and-half. Parsley. We considered adding a bit of curry to this at home, but it was too good the way it was. A bowl of the chowder with rolls or fresh bread made a fine luncheon.

YANKEE CHOWDER

This may horrify the New England purist, but it is very satisfactory at Christmas or at any other time of year.

In 3 cups of salted water, cook 2 cups of diced potatoes, 1 cup of sliced onions, 1 pound of cod or haddock fillets. Add 1 can of creamed corn, as many minced clams as you wish, 1½ quarts of milk, 1 tablespoon of sugar, and pimientos, and simmer. Sprinkle with chopped chives or parsley when serving.

RHODE ISLAND TOADS

These can be served with chowder.

Mix 1 cup each of corn meal and flour with 2 teaspoons of baking powder, 1 egg, salt (sugar is optional). Add enough milk to work this into a dough, and make walnut-sized portions. Drop them into deep fat. These can be kept warm in the oven or reheated. I expect they are a New England version of the Hush Puppies of the South, for which my books give no recipe. Maybe they are like Vermont Dog Supper—everyone knows how to make them.

LIMPING SUSAN

For other Christmas Count teams with more time as they straggle wearily in, you can offer Limping Susan and Hopping John, both of which are Soul Foods and sturdy. When I lived in Florida, I used them a lot for wet and weary men coming in from the Everglades.

Fry a big eggplant. Ha. I don't know what you add to this.

My file card has vanished (if you could see my worktable, you would understand why). Probably, calling on my memories of Soul Food, it is eggplant with rice and beans, onions and peppers. Simple fare from plantation gardens. Sausage or pork, if available. A nice name, though. A sibling to Hopping John.

Aha, I have found Susan. Misfiled. (How could that happen?) Not too different from the above.

Fry an eggplant with bacon, drain off the grease, add 1 cup each of water, rice, tomatoes; and season. Okra adds fine flavor to this, ham can replace the bacon. Cook until the rice is done. And if you need luck or extra nourishment, toss in toward the end a handful of those lucky black-eyed peas (cooked).

HOPPING JOHN

For New Year's luck.

This is based on those lucky peas, 2 cups of them soaked in 5 cups of water overnight. In the morning, bring them to a boil, adding more water if necessary, then simmer them with lots of onion—1½ cups or more—with garlic, bay leaf, hot peppers. After 1 hour stir, in ½ pound of cubed salt pork, and simmer another hour. You can remove the pork or leave it in. I like to render the salt pork over low heat for a while before I add it—I'm a northerner and don't like greasy food. If the pork chunks are crispy, I leave them in.

RABBIT BAKED BEANS

If any Hopping John is left over, I use it in this recipe.

To 2 cups left over from the Hopping John recipe, above, I add ¼ pound of cheese, 2 heaping tablespoons of chili sauce or my own Tomato Relish (see "Condiments"), a little milk, salt, and mustard. Mash this, and heat it in a double boiler.

If any of *this* is left over, an ancient cookbook I inherited says that it makes good sandwiches.

If you are Christmas Counting in Florida or California, you can set your table with heaping bowls of fruit and simple salads, accompanied by an assortment of dressings and muffins.

FRIED EELS

In Portuguese areas, Fried Eels are a standard Christmas dish, to be found in fish markets. (The eels, that is—*you* do the frying). In the salt pond below my home on Cape Cod, I watch fishermen prodding with long poles from their small boats in December about freshwater springs where eels congregate. Sometimes, packing their pickups by my driveway, they give me one. They bid me cut it, skinned, into 3-inch slices, immerse these in boiling water, drain, wipe, roll them in bread crumbs or flour, and fry them in hot fat.

SPIDER JOHNNYCAKE

I don't suggest eels for Christmas Counters, but if you make them, they should be served with Spider Johnnycake, which I do suggest. This is not made from spiders, but is cooked quickly in a heavy iron skillet (spider).

Use any corn-muffin recipe. Grease the skillet well, heat it, pour in the batter, cover it closely, and cook it on top of the stove for about ½ hour. This tastes even better cooked over coals on a campfire, but a kitchen version will do. Diced bacon, cooked or raw, or ham can be incorporated. Old-fashioned recipes call for bacon drippings instead of oil (which would give more flavor) and for buttermilk. The hotter the pan, the crispier the edges. The same batter is good for muffins with a spoonful of jam placed in their centers before baking.

INDIAN PUDDING

As a transplanted New Englander in Florida, I once set out two large casseroles of Indian Pudding for ornithologists, rangers, and their women. Indian Pudding is good for either lunch or dinner—it's a custard dish. No one would touch it. I had to eat it, indignantly, for a week afterward. What's wrong with Indian Pudding? The colonists and whalers (when they reached home) and loving wives thrived on it. There was no lasagne left by those rangers, though, and very little ham.

Cook until thick 4 cups of milk, ½ cup of corn meal, ⅔ cup of molasses, ½ cup of brown sugar. Add 2 cups cold milk, ½ teaspoon each of cinnamon, cloves, ginger, salt, and 1 cup of raisins or dates. (I doubt the colonists had dates. They did have raisins, though.) Bake the pudding for at least 3 hours at 325°, stirring it two or three times.

WHALERS' CHRISTMAS CURRANT CAKE

Another transplant I offered was made from our great-grandmother's faded notes from Long Island, New York. If it could satisfy whalers, it should be good enough for birdwatchers. My sister on the Pacific coast cooks this, carrying on the family tradition where she can see whales passing in migration from her windows. This is a dense cake, better made in muffin tins.

Cream 1 tablespoon of butter with 1 cup of sugar; add 2 beaten eggs, 1 teaspoon of vanilla, 1 cup of milk, 2 cups of flour, 2 teaspoons each of baking powder and salt, 1 cup of currants. Bake at 350°, and ice it with cream added to powdered sugar a little at a time. Rum or brandy will do, if you forgot to buy cream (or even if you didn't—the cake needs flavoring). Sprinkle with red sugar.

By dark on Christmas Count Night, when the teams assemble to report their tallies, they have been drinking coffee all day, they are in the mood for something more revivifying. The ladles and bowls, the mugs that adorn festive tables after a Christmas Count, you will find in the section on drinks.

Fish

My visitors expect fish. They love to stop at a Cape Cod fish store on the way home from birding to pick out our dinner. I've had to learn to make a few dishes I can whip up quickly while they are chatting in the living room, taking showers, organizing their notes.

I've never invested in a lobster kettle (I consider lobsters highly overrated except as a time consumer and conversation leveler), so I am spared the trauma of plunging these ungainly crustaceans into boiling water, then having to rush to the Town Dump first thing next morning to be rid of the smelly residues.

Scallops don't need a recipe. Poach them very briefly in butter and white wine.

Clams make fine broth, and the shells are useful to crush on your paths, but all you are really eating is steamed stomachs and melted butter—we can skip those, too. They are good chopped in a chowder with milk and onion, seasoning, potato, and a little flour for thickening. The real fun of clams is in digging them.

Oysters are marvelous if someone else is willing to prowl the mud flats, find them, open them. All you need is lemon juice or a tangy sauce to dip them in. Or you can place them on their half shells, sprinkle them with seasoned bread crumbs, and run them under the broiler. That's the best, in my opinion, but a lot of trouble.

Mussels I'll accept—no mud, no cut feet or fingers, just a stroll in the clear air, looking out over blue water, two or three of us together getting our feet wet at the tidal edges, skirting rocks, working our way around trees blown down or carried in by a winter storm; stopping to look at shore birds scurrying over the sand, to analyze the species of terns dipping and diving. All you need do is pluck a clump of them from the rocks, being sure they are still partially covered by the tide, pop them into a plastic bag, roll this up, and carry it as you go back to your car, under your arm as if it were a sweater or packet of lunch (which it soon will be). Keep an eye out for a vigilant shellfish warden, though, because now that mussels have become a commercial product as the price of more popular seafoods has soared, their beds are protected. You must compete for the big ones with oystercatchers, who rise before you do, pry open the shells, and eat them, salty, sandy, and probably delicious, on the spot. Bring your mussels home, discard those with broken or open shells, scrub them well; then steam them, covered, in white wine and chopped garlic over high heat until the shells open—6 to 8 minutes. Shake the kettle once or twice to make sure they are well distributed. Again, you are eating stomachs, but they are bigger. I ignore this as I dip them in butter.

The only chowder recipe I've seen for them is really more of a vegetable stew of tomatoes, onions, carrots, celery, garlic, herbs, and seasoning, with mussels, steamed and added at the end with their liquor, scalded cream, and a small pinch of butter, a large pinch of Madeira. In Spain, this would go over vermicelli or its equivalent, which isn't my idea of chowder at all, though I expect it makes a good, filling meal. You'd get squid on top of this, too.

BELIZEAN CHOWDER

In the tropics, chowder is apt to incorporate several kinds of seafood. Diane Weyer, in Belize, takes tourists and shifts from the British army stationed there, to which she is a consultant, caving. She also writes thrillers about a lady assassin. In her spare time, she, with her mother Dora, a well-known naturalist, has provided sustenance on my five trips to Belize. She offers the following, which would be equally suitable wherever conch is available and can have other fish as well. Clams *can* be substituted for conch, but their taste is stronger— use only half as much, she says. She didn't serve our group of researchers from the Manomet Bird Observatory this when we stayed with her at Parrots' Wood. We were far from the coast, and tapir, deer, and paca were more readily available.

"Put a pound each of red snapper, grouper, lobster, and conch, cut up," she orders, "in a big kettle with two pounds each of potatoes and onions, also cut up. Salt and white pepper to taste, enough dried parsley—that's important. No, I never measure—until it looks right. A really big spoonful. Add sugar—maybe two tablespoons—one-half teaspoon each of cinnamon and nutmeg, black pepper. Cook this on a slow fire until the potatoes are tender, then add a tablespoon or so of butter, enough flour to thicken, and evaporated milk—that makes the chowder thick. With this go garlic bread and salad greens, if the local animals have left us any."

ELEANOR'S CHOWDER

"Are we going to have chowder for supper tonight?" Eleanor's young grandchildren demand even before they have struggled out of their car and carried their mother's bags into the house. They fetch poles and nets from a closet, race to the beach, set out in the small dory their grandfather had made for them to catch fish for chowder.

Eleanor lives on a bluff, her rooms looking out over a wide bay to a barrier beach and the Atlantic Ocean. Buffleheads and mergansers, cormorants, mallards, and Canada geese swim below her windows. At dusk, rivers of gulls fly over the blue water in irregular strands, calling, their tilted wings pink and ivory and gold in sunset light. Their talking and movement comes into her bedroom at night.

The chowder her small fishermen clamor for is made, like all good fish chowders, with salt pork—2 or 3 tablespoons of crisps she has rendered in a heavy skillet over low heat. She takes these out, sautés 3 or 4 medium onions in the rendered fat, boils new potatoes in their skins or, if these are out of season, other thin-skinned ones. In as little water as possible until they are not really done but almost so. Then she adds 2 pounds of white-fleshed fish—whatever the children catch— to the water and covers this for a few minutes, letting both fish and potatoes steam until they are done. She flours the salt pork and onions lightly to thicken the chowder, then adds 3 cups of milk with as much half-and-half as is necessary. She doesn't like her chowder thin. It is to be a whole meal, served with biscuits and salad.

PILOT BISCUITS

We searched our old cookbooks in vain for a recipe for pilot biscuits. The best we could come up with was one which calls for 1 cup of flour mixed with ½ cup each of milk and water. You beat this like hell (pardon, but it needs firmness in understanding), drop the dough by spoonfuls on a hissing-hot heavy pan, and bake them in a preheated oven at 450°. Turn down after 20 minutes to 350°. If you use whole-wheat flour, these are called Fadges.

CHOCOLATE-CHIP COOKIES

If you don't like Eleanor's Chowder, you can try the directions for chocolate-chip cookies taped to her wall by the children.

Melt 12 ounces of chocolate chips in a double boiler with ½ cup (1 stick, the children have written in) of margarine or butter. Add 1 cup of flour, 1 can of sweetened condensed milk, 1 tablespoon of rum or amaretto (this is underlined), 1 teaspoon of vanilla, 1 cup of broken pecans. Bake at 350°.

FRIED GRASSHOPPERS

If you don't like Eleanor's cookies, you can experiment with Fried Grasshoppers, a common dish where she lived on the Solomon Islands. Pigs had more protein but were scarce; grasshoppers were abundant. They are a pale, bright green, she says, 6 to 8 inches long, 6 of them quite adequate for a meal. The local children caught them for her. She removed the wings, fried the bodies in a heavy skillet, ate them with rice and a type of wild spinach that grew up into trees like ivy. Cooked, grasshoppers look like shrimp and are tasty, she claims.

Then there are conventional fish dishes. (We were talking about fish. Remember?)

FISH, NEW JERSEY STYLE

Red snapper is best.

Put fish fillets in a buttered pan, spread their tops with bread crumbs moistened with lemon juice or white wine and a little oil, season them with thyme. A refinement is to top this with canned artichoke hearts, halved. Bake the fillets until the fish flakes.

FISH, FLORIDA STYLE

Any kind will do.

Spread fillets in a large, shallow greased pan, and layer over them vegetables ad lib—onion, carrots, broccoli, peppers, green peas or beans, but always a few sliced tomatoes. Top this with bread crumbs or wheat germ or sesame seeds, and Parmesan. Bake the fillets until done. This will depend upon the thickness of both fish and vegetable layers.

PORTUGUESE FISH

Marinate overnight (or while you are out checking ducks on the river) fillets of cod in 1 cup of wine vinegar, 2 cups of water, minced garlic, paprika, ½ teaspoon of red pepper, salt, crushed bay leaves. These can be baked or grilled or broiled, brushing them occasionally with the marinade.

PORTUGUESE FISH STEW

This is like a traditional South American goat stew with fish substituted for the goat.

To 1 sliced onion and 1 garlic clove, minced and sautéed, add 2 pounds of fresh or canned tomatoes, 3 cups or less of water, 4 cups of peeled pumpkin or winter squash, 2 cups of corn. Cook for 15 minutes or until the pumpkin is tender, add 2 pounds of fish, cook 5 to 8 minutes longer. Zucchini can be used instead of pumpkin. This stew will keep, refrigerated, for 3 days and should fill 7 bowls. Depending on the size of your bowls—

NORTHWEST FISH CHOWDER

A version of the above.

Cook until they are soft 1 chopped onion and 1 cup of zucchini or squash in ½ cup of oil. Add 1 can of tomatoes, 2 cups of tomato juice, ⅓ cup of white wine, salt, basil, a dash of Tabasco or hot peppers. Simmer this for 15 minutes, add 1½ pounds of cut-up fish, simmer 5 minutes longer.

Favas (horse beans, but you can ignore that name) are large, protein-full beans like our limas. They go well with either the Portuguese Fish Stew or the Northwest Fish Chowder. Or use them as you would limas.

FISHERMAN'S STEW

To 2 pounds of fish, sliced potatoes, onions, garlic, parsley, coriander, add 1 large can of stewed tomatoes and 1 cup of dry wine. "Cook until done," my fisherman told me. "It depends some on the fish." Serve this with crusty rolls, corn bread, or biscuits.

FISH WITH SHRIMP SOUP

There are three versions of this, all using undiluted canned shrimp soup. One reached me from Boston, one from Vermont, one from Arizona, where I wouldn't expect fish to be a staple. Accidentally one night, Jeannette and I worked out a great improvement on the first two, which we heartily recommend.

Version 1. (Practically instant, no preparation.) Line a baking pan with ⅓ can of shrimp soup, the best you can find. Scatter seasoned bread crumbs on this, place squares of haddock or some other meaty fish on top, then cover the fish with more soup and crumbs. Bake for 20 minutes or more, depending on the thickness of your squares. The soup gets pleasantly crusty.

Version 2. (Equally simple.) Follow the directions for version 1, only use fillets of haddock or flounder (your fish store may sell the latter as sole, but usually it's flounder). Roll the fillets around seasoned crumbs, toothpick each firmly to hold its shape. Dill goes very well with both of these.

Improvement on the above. I was spending the night with my friend Jeannette on my way to give a seminar in New Hampshire. She had asked Susie and Paul Brooks for cocktails. What could I take worthy of these three of my favorite people? I rummaged about in my freezer until I found a pot of Crab Dip I had made for a cocktail party of my own; the dip had turned out too liquid. This had miffed me, I had bought the most expensive crab for the occasion, so I had stashed it away for future use. It would thaw on my 100-mile drive to Boston; I could thicken it there with something. Of course, when I reached Jeannette's, I was late, she had her hors d'ouevres prepared, we forgot the crab until I came into her kitchen to perch on a stool and watch her prepare our supper. While she rolled her fillets, tails first, around their stuffing, I opened the can of shrimp soup. My eye fell upon the crab dip, still thawing gently on the counter. I don't really like shrimp soup all by itself. Why not, I suggested, mix my crab into it, see what we came up with?

It was marvelous. Jeannette looked at me in horror when I confessed that I didn't know how I'd made it. There must be a recipe somewhere. We searched her cookbooks; their recipes called for catsup or chili sauce, onion juice, mustard. "No," I said weakly. "I would have started with half a pound of crab— that's what I'd bought. Maybe I'd have put mayonnaise with this, a little lemon juice, a small package of softened cream cheese, though maybe I had cottage cheese in the fridge that I used instead; sour cream—I always have some of that that needs to be used. Probably I put in too much, that's what made my dip so thin. A couple of my guests picked out crab-meat hunks with a toothpick, but the rest sensibly left it alone. I don't *know* how much of anything. When I get home I'll experiment. Half a cup of mayonnaise (my own mayonnaise), half a cup of sour cream? The cheese to thicken it? The juice of half a lemon? I must have a recipe somewhere." Only when I reached home, I found I hadn't. Cottage cheese (maybe ½ cup?) would be easier for mix than the cream cheese—fine curd.

However it comes out it will be a terrific improvement over just plain shrimp soup in the two versions above.

Note: I spent a lot of time looking for that crab-meat recipe. I should have looked in this—my own—cookbook. Painfully working my way through the copy-editing of a woman far more thorough and patient than I am, there, on page 247, it was! Joyfully, I called Jeannette. "Not too different from what you figured out," she said comfortingly. (I separate my friends into those who comfort and those who always tell the truth. I need both kinds.) "Hurry back, and we'll cook that dish again."

Version 3. (More elaborate, but worth the trouble.) Blend 1 can of the soup or lobster bisque (aaaah) with 3 tablespoons of flour, and stir in ¼ cup each of milk and white wine. Cook the sauce, stirring it, until it is thick. Then add 1 ounce of slivered mozzarella, a bit of garlic salt, Worcestershire sauce, and minced parsley. Combine this with 1 or 2 pounds of cod fillets that have been cut into chunks, brought to a boil with a small onion slice, a little lemon juice, and water to cover, simmered until the fish flaked, and drained. Put this in a buttered baking dish, and bake it for 20 minutes at 375°. Then spread over the top of the dish ¼ cup of melted butter, about 1 cup of bread crumbs, 2 tablespoons of Parmesan, ½ teaspoon of paprika, and dill. Bake the fish 10 minutes longer. This dish can be frozen and then reheated another day.

MARGIE'S FISH SKILLET

A one-dish quickie.

Layer 2 cups each of thinly sliced raw potatoes and ½ cup of shortening with lots of chopped dill and a package each of frozen green beans and peas. Spread 1 pound of fish fillets over this, and add ¼ cup each of water and lemon juice or white wine. Cover, and simmer for 20 minutes. Garnish with lemon slices.

JEANNETTE'S FLOUNDER FLORENTINE

"Only it should be sole," she apologizes. "Like you, I think often what they sell for sole is flounder anyway."

When I must go to Boston, Jeannette beds me in a study overflowing with books, papers, and other impedimenta of a professional still never too busy to take care of friends.

"I give you Flounder Florentine so often," she apologizes again, "because it's so easy, and I like spinach. You can make it early in the day, too, so you can enjoy a sherry in the living room with your guests." She moves briskly about her kitchen, handing me scallions and a cutting board, deciding on a dessert. "It's delicate; it goes well with parslied new potatoes. When there are four of us, like tonight, I use two packages of frozen spinach to one-and-a-half pounds of flounder fillets." She is draining the cooked spinach, squeezing it dry. She thickens 1½ cups of sour cream with flour—"about two to three tablespoons"—gathers the scallions I have chopped. "I want some tops, please," she demands, also passing me parsley to chop, adds a spoonful of salt and some lemon juice to the cream, mixes about half of this with the spinach, spreads it deftly over the bottom and sides of a shallow baking dish I've watched her use for years. The fillets get layered over the spinach, then covered with the rest of the cream mixture and dotted with an ample amount of butter. "Real butter," she says severely, knowing my habits. "We can put this in the fridge now, cook it while we sit in the other room. It will take about twenty-five minutes" at 375°.

HALIBUT AND LIMA-BEAN CASSEROLE

I suppose this is my favorite fish recipe because I have made it so often that I don't have to think about it and because it is hearty enough not to demand side dishes. Besides, I'm a lima-bean fan; I welcome any excuse to have them.

Sauté 1 garlic clove and 1 small onion, both cut up, with mushrooms—¼ pound or more. Add 2 tablespoons of flour, blend, add 1 16-ounce can of tomatoes, 2 tablespoons of vinegar or white wine, 1 tablespoon of Worcestershire sauce, salt, pepper, thyme or dill, and 1 package of frozen lima beans. Cook the mixture for about 5 minutes or until the beans separate, then pour it over the fish, which has been placed in a greased pan. Bake at 400° for 30 minutes or until the fish flakes.

While I am doing this, one guest puts together a green salad, another slices homemade bread, a third sets the table. I don't have to work in my kitchen alone. I use cookies for dessert—and fruit.

CRAB CAKES

When Chan Robbins and Gladys Cole and, over weekends, a motley crew of volunteers were working the famous North Ocean City U.S. Fish & Wildlife Birdbanding Station (now become tennis courts, condominiums, and a marina), the nearest motel was 10 miles north in Delaware, and there were no convenient restaurants (or we couldn't afford them—I've forgotten which). Chan would excuse me each night (I was the lowest on the totem pole) in time to reach a small shop where we had a standing order for cooked crab cakes and a pail of coleslaw. It was a race always to get there before eight, when the shop closed. The owner became interested in us, amused by our steady diet, and tolerant of my tardiness.

You might think I would have had my fill of crab cakes. But when the North Ocean City Station closed and I moved my gear to Dottie Mendinhall's on Chesapeake Bay, I made them myself as a special treat for visitors (and me). Dottie would send me in at dusk to cook while she banded the last catbirds and white-throated sparrows. She didn't care, really, what we ate as long as she didn't have to fuss with it.

For 6 people, I would mix 1 pound of crab meat with soft bread crumbs (the amount of crumbs depended upon how many unexpected visitors we might have). This would be tossed with 2 tablespoons of oil, 2 beaten eggs, 1 teaspoon each of salt and Worcestershire sauce, and onion-soup mix that had been sitting in ¼ cup of sour cream or sherry. I dropped this mixture by spoonfuls into hot butter and cooked the cakes until they were golden brown on each side. I could whip up biscuits (they're quick, take about as much time as the crab cakes) and serve them with honey and whatever vegetable we might have had. We would sit long over coffee until Dottie snapped her whip and we reached for the day's record sheets.

CRAB SAINT ANTHONY

If you add black olives to the above crab-cake recipe and put the mixture into a casserole dish, you can call it Crab Saint Anthony. Add sautéed mushrooms, dust with paprika, pour ½ cup of dry sherry over the top, and bake at 400°. Shrimp can be substituted for crab, but not by me. I have a special relationship with Saint Anthony. He finds all my lost articles for me—car keys, once a misplaced child at a World's Fair—I wouldn't insult him with shrimp.

CATFISH STEW AND STRIPED BASS

(But not together.)

The Wheeler National Wildlife Refuge in northern Alabama is famous for a list that runs to 300 birds, many thousands of birdwatchers who come to it, and its Christmas Count. The manager, Tom Akeson, is also famous. One of his attributes is his way with Catfish Stew as well as Striped Bass. He cooks the bass with mustard and Tabasco—not too much of either, I'd judge. Bass is no longer plentiful enough where I live for me to experiment, but if you can get it more easily, try this broiled. I wrote to him to ask for details, but rangers and refuge managers and biologists (who seem to be the kind of men I know best) are busy; they don't always get around to answering unimportant letters.

Northerners seem to think catfish ignoble food, and certainly the fish are full of bones. But so are shad, which those same Northerners happily accept in spring, so why not eat catfish, which are even more delicious? I miss catfish country, and netting at night for shrimp by flashlight in the waterways of the Everglades, and conch from the turquoise seas off the Florida Keys, the Caribbean island, the Gulf of Honduras. What am I doing here on a small salt pond, watching menhaden jump under the shadows of great blue herons trailing their long legs down the river? Menhaden are an essential food for bigger fish; I get to eat them only secondhand.

Bread

My bread isn't better than any one else's, often not as good. I've been making it since before many of my competitors were born, so I don't need to measure, don't get upset if no two batches come out alike. You don't *have* to have homemade bread—markets sell a variety of shapes and sizes, textures, colors, ingredients—but making it is fun, foolproof, far less expensive, fills your home with delicious aromas, and produces a treat rather than just a staff of life taken for granted on the table or a station-wagon tailgate. If it doesn't turn out as you had hoped, you call it "peasant bread" (it will disappear equally as fast). Men slice it thicker and eat it faster than women do, so one loaf is impractical. Make four, five, six at a time—it's no more work.

Basic directions are in any cookbook and on sacks of flour. After you master one—even before—start substituting or adding. I use half white flour to keep my dough from being too heavy, always 1 egg (maybe 2), always a double amount of yeast if I am using dark flour. I toss into the warm liquid ½ cup each of quick oats, soy and or buckwheat flakes, rye, a little corn meal, some wheat germ, adding 1 extra cup of liquid for these. Always bran, ½ to 1 full cup for a rich flavor. Powdered milk. You can add wheat berries (previously cooked to tender), mashed potatoes. You can use vegetable stock, water, or milk. You see why I say bread is a creative process? In some countries, yeast is sold by the pound, which gives you an indication of what the bread consumption must be in homes where the kitchen is a woman's career. I use molasses instead of sugar— ½ cup.

Sometimes I wait until the yeast mixture of liquids and ingredients that are soaking bubble. If I am in a hurry, I add right away whatever flours are handy until I have dough stiff enough to knead—that is, to push and pull and thump, roll into a ball, push and pull and roll some more. Kneading is relaxing, sensuous. It's like handling clay or a baby. Something is being created under your hands, your mind drifts off, love flows through your fingers. How can a baker with his electric mixer and measuring tools incorporate this peace into his products? Days when I am cranky or hurried, my loaves reflect this. Which is more valuable to my family, to my friends—more valuable to *me*, really—the time I spend at my typewriter clacking its keys or the time I spend in my kitchen, dreaming, inventing, singing as I oil my pans? All right, I'm old-fashioned. But I notice that more and more men, harassed by obligations, by office pressures, have turned to making bread weekends or, if they get home early enough, to punching together a dough that can be baked for breakfast the next morning. Homemade bread is perhaps a symbol of a day when life was more leisurely. In a way, it's a commitment—to your spouse, your children, yourself. With cheese, fruit, and wine, it is a meal you can't buy, carrying with it, as you break its crust on a picnic, the aroma of home.

FIVE- (OR SEVEN-) GRAIN BREAD

"If you don't put in just *one* of your bread recipes, I'll kill you and blackball your books," says my friend Jane. I count on Jane: she is reliable, a pillar of our town, gives great dinner parties. She is a breadmaker in her own right, she doesn't need any instruction. But I don't want her blackballing me. So here is my recipe, Jane—no exact measurements, but the best I can come up with. It's what I make the most.

Into 3 cups of really warm liquid—water, vegetable stock (if I have any), potato water are all fine—I set to soak 1 cup of bran, ½ cup each of powdered milk, rolled oats, wheat flakes, soy flakes, wheat germ, sometimes (but not necessarily) cooked wheat berries, sometimes corn meal (but it's gritty). As this cools, I add salt and ½ cup of molasses. I shake 2 packets of yeast (2 tablespoons, if it comes from a bottle) into ½ cup of warm water measured into my unwashed molasses measure. Yeast likes that touch of sweet to start it rising. When the yeast foams, I add it to the mix in the bowl, being sure the contents are warm but not hot. Sometimes I let all this foam a little while I make beds or a telephone call, do dishes. But don't try to write a letter; you'll forget to return to the kitchen. Then I add 2 eggs—well, maybe 1 (it depends upon how many I have). You don't need to let your bowl of ingredients start to foam. I am more apt to stir in right away 3 cups of whole-wheat flour, then unbleached white flour until the dough becomes too stiff to stir and turn with my big wooden spoon. I punch the dough down in the bowl with my knuckles, turn it, adding more flour as needed, dump it out onto a floured board, and continue to punch and turn and add, knead and roll, until the dough no longer sticks to the board, is smooth to my hands, feels alive under them.

Some cooks consider this onerous and use an electric mixer,

but I enjoy it. My conscious mind tunes out; ideas and emotions surface to color my day. I am looking out a window at bushes coming into bloom or berry, or bending under snow. Birds dart to my feeder, drink from a pottery bowl, look back through the window at me. I oil the bread bowl, drop my ball of dough back in, turn it to distribute the oil, cover it with wax paper and a dish towel to keep its warmth and moisture in. In really cold weather, I set it in a barely warmed oven. But if I don't see the bowl, I may forget it, so I'm more apt to put it on the floor where heat comes out from under a cupboard. If the dough feels heavy, as when I use rye flour or too much whole wheat, I can punch it down after it doubles and let it rise again. No problem. I go about my other businesses. The dough will double faster each time, but you can always punch it again if it rises too much, looks unhappy. Finally, I drop it onto a floured board, knead it a little more, shape it, place the loaves on a cookie sheet so I don't have all those pans to deal with, let them rise a final time, and bake them at 350° for about 40 minutes. The books say to preheat the oven, but often I don't.

There are refinements, like using proper bread pans (which give tidier shapes) or glazing the unbaked loaves lightly with water or egg white and water (I *do* mean lightly, unless you want a cement crust), then sprinkling the glaze with sesame seeds. But basically, Jane, this is *it*. And it won't ever come out twice the same. Does this matter? Yes. If I use too many rolled oats, it doesn't slice neatly for sandwiches.

People write books on breadmaking. I look through them. I'm trying to learn how to make black bread, but they don't tell me. Not a way that works for me, anyway. Add Postum is one advice. Add a square of baking chocolate and two spoons full of instant coffee is another. Toast leftover bread crumbs until they are black, and incorporate these, I was told by a thick-waisted, middle-European woman who obviously lived on a bread diet. Only I don't have bread crumbs—they have gone into soup or been shaken out for blue jays and sparrows.

That's *my* bread I've offered you—and Jane. Since you may not like it, I'll offer a few others. I'm sure they are all in cookbooks, but different.

PANETTONE

After he retired, my husband worked with international trade fairs for our government, so we traveled a lot. We were in Milan several times, but the one I remember most vividly was an Easter weekend, three particular scenes. The first, because it was daily, was an astonishing file of tourists for such an hour creeping along the roofs and ledges of the great cathedral, peering down at the unpaid-for bonus of me performing my matutinal exercises by our long window. What were they doing, filing around up there before seven o'clock in the morning? If I pulled shut our heavy window draperies, I had no light and, more important, no air. I ignored my spectators. They would never recognize me when, clothed and hatted, I sallied onto the streets at a reasonable hour.

The second scene *was* a scene, when an innocent young bus-boy in a famous restaurant near the Galleria took a stack of warming plates from under the cart where the maître d' (that appellation should be in Italian, but I never learned much Italian—we moved around too fast. Besides, unlike the Span-ish—we were in Spain a lot, too—when I mixed up my verbs and tenses, I found Italians stonily rude, unlovable, so I became discouraged. This sentence is too long.) was making Crêpes

Suzette for our table of dignitaries, from whom he was expecting extra payment for the dramatic flourishes and flames he was putting on. At the crucial moment when he reached for warm plates—his pans ablaze—the plates were *gone!* Italians are emotional. The drama was magnificent, better than the Crêpes. Warmer.

Third and daily were my saunters along streets with astonishing numbers of bakeries and patisseries (whatever names Italians call them by—pasticceria?) Their windows glowed with Easter delicacies, chocolate in a myriad of enticing displays and—in almost an equal number of rough-hatted sizes and fragrances—an Italian Easter staple, panettone. I became an addict, twice a day eating individual ones accompanied by hot chocolate with whipped cream. No wonder my dresses ceased to fit, in spite of those morning exercises. Panettone is to the Milanese what Easter lilies are to us, blooming seasonally in every window. Actually, it is nothing but a sweet bread, anise-flavored, larded with golden raisins and candied fruit, but always baked in the round—in tins, saucepans, deep molds, whatever—the crown tops swollen and golden. Varied sizes for varied pocketbooks. People ate them on the spot, carried them off under their arms. Mostly men, I noticed, as gifts for the "little woman" at home, celebrating the holy day much as here we latchkey slaveys are given candy and flowers.

For a time, I collected recipes for panettone. They averaged out to a dough made of ½ cup of scalded milk cooled to room temperature, to which is added 1 yeast cake dissolved in ¼ cup of warm water, ½ to 1 cup of sugar, 2 to 4 beaten eggs, ½ to 1 cup of butter, 1½ teaspoons of salt, ¾ teaspoon of anise extract (that's essential). There has to be flour in this (I forgot to write it on my recipe card)—about 5 cups. Beat the dough thoroughly. It should be soft, too soft to knead. Let it rise until it doubles in bulk. In the second kneading, incorporate 1 cup of chopped candied fruit, with lots of citron (1 cup, anyway), 1 cup of golden raisins, grated lemon rind, nutmeg. Let the dough rise again. (If you want, you can punch it down again with your fist, turn it over, let it rise a third time. This is optional.) Punch it down with floured hands, and separate it into greased "pans." To make individual small loaves such as the ones I bought for lunch, you could use custard cups or frozen-juice cans. For bigger loaves, I've used 16-ounce fruit or vegetable tins, coffee tins (yes, I've really made it; it's rather fun, but be sure you grease your pans well or the loaves won't come out). An angel-cake pan (tube pan) works well but isn't Italian. Slash the tops of the panettones and brush them lightly with melted butter *before* baking them, or glaze them with 1 egg beaten with 2 tablespoons of water *after* baking them. Be aware that small tins bake faster than large ones! Bake at 350°.

In Poland, this is called Przekladaniec. Stewed apricots and/or prunes replace the candied cherries and pineapple.

Now you are on your own.

DAILY BREAD

From Germany.

Spicy Rye Bread involves a trip to a health-food store, but that's how you keep these interesting shops in business. If they don't have fennel and anise seeds, see if they have the flavoring or use caraway seeds. Don't worry if this bread doesn't rise high—it shouldn't. Roll it small and thin to use for cocktail dips, and bake it on a cookie sheet at 350°.

To 1½ cups of lukewarm water or vegetable stock, add 2 yeast cakes, ½ cup of molasses, salt, 1 tablespoon of grated orange rind (optional), 2 tablespoons of oil, 1 tablespoon each of fennel seeds and anise seeds. When this foams, beat in 2 cups of rye flour, ½ cup of soy flour, 2 cups each of whole-wheat and white flours, and ¼ cup of dried milk. Mix the ingredients, knead, let rise, knead at least once more, shape into long rolls, and let rise again. It's a heavy bread, so I often give it a second rising before shaping it into loaves and placing them on a cookie sheet dusted with corn meal. If your loaves are thin, remember they won't take as long to bake. Fine sliced for cocktail dips.

AMERICAN BUTTERY CRUSTY ROLLS

I don't really like these, but my family does. At least it's quick. Don't use an 8″ × 8″ pan; it's too small. Or do, but reserve some of the dough to bake in custard cups.

Heat 1 cup of milk, 1 tablespoon of honey, 1 tablespoon of butter; then cool the mixture to room temperature, and add 1 tablespoon of yeast. When this bubbles, add 1½ cups of white flour, and beat the dough until it is elastic. Let it rise for 30 minutes. Melt 5 tablespoons of butter in your pan (save a little). (My original directions called for a total of 8 tablespoons of butter. I've cut this back some, but maybe not enough. Or you may like the rolls more buttery.) Drop equal portions of the dough into the pan, allowing room for them to spread, then brush the tops with the reserved butter. You can let these rise a bit or put them right away into a cold oven. They will rise as the oven warms. Bake at 400° for about 30 minutes, and serve hot.

PARKER HOUSE ROLL DOUGH

Very useful.

When I was a child growing up near Boston, Parker House Rolls at one point became a topic of conversation. Puzzled, I inquired about them. So my father took me to the city to visit the famous hotel for which they were named. Whether it was the unfamiliar formality of a city restaurant, an elderly waiter hovering over me, holding my chair, laying a napkin on my lap with a flourish, or the unexpected parental attention I don't know, but after I was married I made the famous rolls, which are in every cookbook, a feature of our parties. These days I substitute some whole-wheat flour (about one-third) for white. One advantage to the recipe is that it is *big*. I make as many rolls as I need, cutting them big with a doughnut cutter or small with a jar top dipped in flour, then knead the leftover cuttings with more dough, roll this out, spread it with soft butter, brown sugar, walnuts (you don't need to measure), and make cinnamon rolls. Or I use the leftover dough, also spread with butter, sugar, and cinnamon, to make small loaves to give away.

When I cook like this, I lose my appetite and lose weight. It's more effective than going on a diet.

FRENCH BREAD

There's a recipe further on, Molly's Spinach Dip, that goes with drinks at cocktail parties or can be used for a summer luncheon. It calls for French Bread. This comes at the bakery in loaves much to long to please me. Half of it gets wasted, goes out to the bird feeder. I decided to make my own—small ones. This proved easy. All it really is is yeast and flour. You can eat it plain with butter, breaking it off in hunks, or with cheese, or with garlic or herb butter. Heat the bread in foil just before serving it. I use Fanny Farmer's recipe (more or less) because her measurements mostly are in multiples of 2. I don't have to look them up each time.

Dissolve 2 tablespoons of dry yeast in 2 cups of warm water mixed with 2 tablespoons of sugar. When this bubbles, add 4 tablespoons of melted shortening or oil and 2 cups of flour, and beat thoroughly. Add 1 tablespoon of salt and 3 cups more of flour (you have to remember these figures). Knead the dough on a floured board, let it rest for 10 minutes, knead it some more, adding flour with your hands until the dough is elastic and doesn't stick to the board. Return to a greased bowl, cover, and let it rise in a warm place until it doubles. Knead it again, shape it into small loaves of the size *you* want, and set on a greased cookie sheet sprinkled with corn meal. If you wish, you can glaze the loaves—gently—with an egg white beaten with 1 tablespoon of water, and sprinkle them with poppy or sesame seeds. Bake at 375°. If you want a thick crust, bake at a lower temperature. Be sure to bake long enough (I can't tell you how long that is—it depends on loaf size and on your oven). On a cookie sheet, the loaves will spread and be flatter than store ones. But they taste and pull into hunks the same whether they are narrow or flat.

There seem to be as many opinions and variations on French Bread as there are happy memories of France. My own opinion is that it is easy to serve, is a good conversation piece, and lacks the nourishment of "honest" bread, although it can be made with sourdough or rye flour, according to some books, and, I would think (I haven't tried it—next time), with whole-wheat flour.

FRENCH ONION BREAD

Use the above recipe, only stir a package of dried onion-soup mix into the hot water and let it sit a bit before you continue. Add 2 additional tablespoons of sugar and 2 of Parmesan.

Condiments

The Basics

HORSERADISH

Traveling on a Japanese train once—comfortable, clean, big windows (also clean)—vendors at noon brought trays of wooden boxes. I found the contents I sampled interesting, if often mysterious. At the end of our meal, I dug into a flat, round box that appeared to be a cheese, perhaps a sweet cake, and took a big spoonful. The top of my head blew off, my eyes streamed. Now, every once in awhile to amuse myself and remember the Virtue of Caution, I buy a horseradish, peel and grate the root, and mix it with vinegar. It is good (a little, a very little) added to cocktail and fish sauces, to mayonnaise, to warmed jelly as a meat sauce. It is also a diuretic, a stimulant, and a remedy for worms. It cures scurvy and is better for coughs than a mustard plaster. You should grate it fresh each time you use it, but I refrigerate it with a lemon slice on top, hoping this will keep it from turning bitter.

MUSTARD

Matthew (13:32) wrote of it: "The least of all seeds: but when it is grown, it is the greatest among herbs, and becometh a tree, so that the birds of the air come and lodge in the branches thereof." Folk medicine thought it an antidote for scorpion bites.

My mustard recipe is tattered; many friends have coped it. It's so foolproof and evidently so good that I don't understand why it isn't kept in the fridge as automatically as milk and butter. I soak 4 ounces of dry mustard powder overnight (or for at least 8 hours) in 1 cup of vinegar—herb, wine, or cider. Then I cook this in a double boiler with 2 beaten eggs and 1 cup of sugar, stirring the mixture a bit at first so the eggs don't curdle, and go about my business. It will be thick enough in 35 to 40 minutes (but I have forgotten it and left it on the stove for an hour or more). It's hotter than the average store mustard, must be refrigerated, and will keep for weeks.

HERB VINEGARS

These are also so easy to make that it's a wonder we ever buy them. Maybe the pretty bottles they come in seduce us. If you have fresh herbs in your garden, simply stuff a large clean jar with them and fill it with heated vinegar—red or white or just cider. Or "borrow" herbs from a friend, buy them at market, or use dried ones (½ cup of dried herbs to 2 cups of vinegar). Cap your bottle tightly, and set it in a dark place for 2 or 3 weeks, giving it a good shake from time to time. You can add crushed garlic or a chili pepper or two. Strain the brew, decant it into attractive bottles, and give them to your friends. (Dill is good for insomnia, you can add to your labels.)

My original instructions came from a friend who received them from an economist who worked at the Library of Congress. She didn't know his political persuasion and said she didn't think it mattered.

HERB-FLAVORED OILS

These are made the same way as the vinegars. Be sure to use good olive oil. If you are giving them away, put a sprig of fresh herbs in each bottle. That goes for Herb Vinegars, too.

SHERRY-PEPPER SAUCE

Also made the same way as the vinegars and oils.

Steep 4 fresh red or green hot peppers and 2 small chili peppers in 2 cups of dry sherry. This will be HOT and, if you don't strain it after about 2 weeks, will get HOTTER. It's a fine addition to soups, stews, marinades, chowders, poached eggs, pan-fried fish. (And to Bloody Mary Soup!)

TOMATO RELISH OR CHILI SAUCE

I have no name for this Fisk concoction, but you will find it all year in quart jars in the back of my fridge, where it keeps very well (no paraffin). It goes into soups, breakfast eggs, casseroles, fried potatoes, sautéed chicken livers, rice, etc. It started in my early Buffalo days, when some mother had to watch the neighborhood children playing in the streets, to referee their games and squabbles. With a wooden bowl I could just curve my arm around and a double-bladed knife, I would sit on the curb chopping celery, peppers, onions, garlic, and tomatoes while I administered Authority, Justice, and First Aid. I never measured, just chopped, added vinegar and sugar—enough vinegar so it wouldn't burn, enough sugar for my taste—and simmered this until it was thick enough or my bedtime. I've been making it ever since. I wouldn't be without those jars to help me through emergencies. But don't get persnickety and want measurements because I can't give you any. Lots of celery. And never put it in a blender—that would take all the fun, lumps, and seeds out of it.

SEASONED SALT

You can buy this, but why not just stand in front of your various herb jars and mix 5 tablespoons of salt, 1 tablespoon each of sugar and paprika, 1 teaspoon each of nutmeg, thyme, oregano, marjoram, celery salt, onion and garlic powders, and dry mustard? Vary this any way you want, and put the money it would cost you at the store into your piggy bank.

MAYONNAISE

This takes all of five minutes unless it's a very hot day, it curdles, and you have to start again, pouring the mix SLOWLY onto an extra egg in the bottom of your blender.

Blend 2 eggs with 4 tablespoons of vinegar (any kind), ½ teaspoon each of salt and dry mustard. Remove the center of the blender cover, and, with the blender growling at you, pour in—very slowly at first—2 cups of salad oil. Toward the end, when the mayonnaise gets really thick, if the oil is no longer being absorbed, stir with a rubber spatula and blend it some more.

There will be a fair amount of mayonnaise left at the bottom of the blender after you have spooned out what you can. Make Dressing of the House. If you just add oil and vinegar (¼ cup of vinegar to ¾ cup of oil) and seasonings to the leftovers, you have a Creamy French Dressing. Add to this a spoonful of sugar or two and poppy seeds, and you have Poppy Seed Dressing. Or add Roquefort or chili sauce. You can keep adding oil and vinegar until you are willing to consign the blender to the dishpan. The Poppy Seed Dressing is great with any kind of seafood salad.

HOLLANDAISE

I don't suppose this is much harder to make than mayonnaise (if you use a blender), but it sounds more complicated and all those calories make me nervous. It's the opposite of mayonnaise in that you keep it Hot; the ingredients for mayonnaise should be Cold. When I make hollandaise in a blender, it always winds up at the bottom (and I'm not mechanical enough to take my blender apart). And because you will need to keep the sauce warm to spread on your fish or vegetables or Eggs Benedict, you may as well make it in a double boiler to begin with. Don't keep it warm too long, though—not more than 1 hour. It can be refrigerated and reheated.

In a double boiler over boiling water, whisk (that means really whisk—with a wire whisk) 3 egg yolks, and keep whisking as you slowly add 3 tablespoons of lemon juice *or* 1 tablespoon of lemon juice and another of dry sherry and another of plain or herb vinegar, ½ teaspoon of fresh chopped dill, a pinch of cayenne, salt. Whisk this until it is smooth and thickens. Then drizzle in, still whisking, ¼ to ½ pound of butter which you have been melting over low heat until, says Ellie of The Sand Dollar, "it is bubbly and smells like toasted nuts but is not brown." (I told you this sounds complicated.) Add that butter very slowly.

The above is for the purist for use on fish, vegetables, Eggs Benedict. But you can also whisk in grated onion, mustard, finely chopped tarragon and parsley—½ teaspoon each of the last three, more of the onion.

After having made it myself once, I now understand why hostesses give me black looks when I politely refuse it at their dinner table.

PESTO

Mary Durant could, I am sure, make a palatable salad of dandelion greens and whatever might be growing on the fringes of her herb garden. This is her recipe for Pesto.

Mix 2 cups of basil that has been moistened with olive oil with 3 garlic cloves, a pinch of salt, 1 cup of Parmesan. Then blend the ingredients into a paste, trickling into it 1½ cups of olive oil.

Mary and her husband Mike Harwood probably feed more intinerant birders than I do and so would use this up quickly. I froze mine in ¼-cup plastic containers and found that it kept well and indefinitely, usefully at hand for soups, salads, and casseroles. If you don't have any of those small containers, order a carry-out dinner from your local Chinese food shop. Their sauces come in them. (A handy size for chopped peppers and mushrooms, too.)

Flowers, Herbs, and Seeds

My dictionary defines a condiment as anything that enhances the flavor of food. If we add herbs and mint and parsley, watercress, sprouts, Jerusalem artichokes, mushrooms, and water chestnuts to our dishes, why not flowers from our garden?

Small nasturtium leaves or seeds are good in soups, on pork, on potato or crab salad. They do well in mayonnaise, with mustard and curry, or with lemon juice and honey. Can be put in a bottle with vinegar, garlic, shallots, and a spoonful of honey for a Flower Vinegar. (Cap the bottle loosely, keep it for 2 to 3 weeks, and add the vinegar to salad dressings.)

A tablespoon of marigold petals can be added to rice, eggs, crab meat or tuna, zucchini, sandwiches, custard, and muffins. I've even been told that a *cupful* of them can be used with venison steak. Marigolds are versatile.

Yarrow *(Achillea)* is a weed (a native flower out of place) that reached this country probably in cattle fodder. It is useful in dried-flower arrangements. It is also used in its place of origin (Europe) as a tea, providing vitamins and minerals. It may be added to beer. The tender young flowers can be put in salads. (I do this with marjoram flowers, too.)

The mint overrunning your garden was thought in the Middle Ages to whiten teeth, heal bites from mad dogs, relieve wasp stings, and repel rats and mice. So you may be doing yourself a favor when you add it to iced tea, salads, and lamb kebab.

Marjoram, the herb of grace. There are two big plants of this in my garden. Birds ignore it, not even slugs like it; but *I* use its small flowers in salads and soups all summer, as well as its leaves. Then I dry some for winter use. Medicine no longer recommends steeping it as a cure for asthma, coronary disease, headaches, and spider bites, but who knows? The Greeks believed that, like parsley, it prevented drunkenness, so marjoram might be useful in these days of drunk-driving laws.

Poppy seeds are only flowers in embryo, but, like sesame

seeds, they have many uses, enhancing vegetables, fish, fruits, salads, breads. Like sesames, they should be toasted for 15 minutes in a 350° oven for the best flavor, unless they are to be used as an excellent topping for casseroles (instead of crumbs) or bread. A particular virtue of poppy seeds is that they are supposed to make you invisible to creditors.

Sesame seeds, like black-eyed peas, bring luck, with the added advantage that they can be used in many ways and all year long (for luck). They add taste to salads, cereals, casseroles, breads, vegetables, and fish. They make a good substitute for walnuts in cookies—½ a cup instead of 1 cup of the nuts. They should be toasted lightly before use, on a flat sheet in a 350° oven. Keep an eye on them—they should be golden, not brown. A friend used to send me a tin of Benne Wafers every year at Christmas. They were thin and crisp and always arrived well crumbled. I would crumble them further and put them on the childrens' puddings or in their breakfast cereal as a substitute for sugar. My friend paid a high price for them, so I didn't tell her this. They came in attractive tins—I still have one in a cupboard.

Preserves

HOT-PEPPER JELLY

You can't be a proper birdwatcher without taking an interest in flowers and seeds, learning what birds eat, which eat what, what your land should provide for them. You aren't a serious birdwatcher—or gardener—unless you are constantly browsing in bookshops, even when fate (or your husband's business) has you living in canyons or the carbon monoxide of a city. The tiny kitchen behind the Francis Scott Key bookshop in Georgetown, Washington, D.C., has given way to progress, its walls now stocked with books instead of pots and jars. Too bad. I'm sure one of the reasons its customers browsed in the salesroom was the variety of fragrances that seeped through the walls from Marty Johnson's cooking. Her specialty was this jelly.

"But it's so easy," she protested when special customers clamored for a jar of it. "All you do is clean the seeds out of enough peppers to make a cupful (you may want to wear rubber gloves, they are really hot—don't rub your eyes). Grind them small, put them in a pot with one-and-one-half cups of vinegar and six-and-one-half cups of sugar. Bring this to a full, rolling boil for one minute, stirring so it won't boil over, then let it cool for five minutes. Add a bottle of Certo, following the directions on the bottle, and stir well. This will make six half-pint jars. Bits of red and green bell pepper are decorative. If you want it hotter, use more hot peppers and fewer bells, and vice versa."

Every year at Christmas, Marty carefully packs a jar for me and sends it to wherever I am living.

As at each Christmas, from Florida comes a jar of Elderberry Jelly from the kitchen of an eminent ornithologist on the staff of the Florida Audubon Society. Elderberry, also often considered a weed, is a large shrub found from New England to south Florida. Its berries are fine in wine, jelly, ale, soups, and— I'm told—as a cure for warts. It is rich in vitamin C. To me it poses an ethical problem. My soil isn't moist enough to

nurture elderberries; I have to thieve mine from roadsides. Should I leave those umbels of small purple fruits for catbirds and thrush, or gather them for jelly and pie? Late in the summer, when the temptation of the fruit is gone, though, I can break a branch to hang over my door. I wonder if Dr. Kale knows that this keeps devils and witches from my home (and jelly shelf)?

RED-PEPPER JAM

Sweet and colorful, only I can't imagine it without just one or two hot peppers in it—for spice.

Clean 12 sweet red peppers, add 1 tablespoon of salt, and let stand overnight. Drain the peppers, then add 2 cups of sugar and 2 cups of vinegar. Stir, heat to boiling, then simmer the mixture until it is thick. Like its hot green twin, it is fine on cream cheese.

Before we get into a discussion of marmalades, let me save you hours of chopping by advising you to put your citrus peels— cut up some, but not much—into a blender with some of the liquid you are using and give them just enough of a whirl to break them into the required small pieces. You can slosh out the blender afterward with juice or water. Waste nothing!

RED-PEPPER MARMALADE

Thinly slice 6 lemons, simmer them for ½ hour, let them sit overnight. Add 4 large sweet red bell peppers, cleaned and minced, 4 small hot peppers, ½ cup of cider vinegar, and 4 cups of sugar. Boil the mixture rapidly until it reaches the jelly stage, stirring it constantly as it thickens. If you want this to be foolproof, you needn't boil it so long. Just add Certo (see directions on the Certo bottle; it saves time and strength). Check the sugar amount.

I am lazy and usually add Certo. If I don't and my products don't jell, I use them in sweet-and-sour sauces or for stewing fruits. Cream cheese is what they are really meant to go with, though.

CALAMONDIN MARMALADE

In subtropical Florida, I planted, nurtured, and gloried in a fragrant small calamondin tree, which rewarded my attentions with two fine crops a year and a sufficient sprinkling of fruit all winter to bless my iced tea and rum drinks. Calamondins are small, thin-skinned citrus—like tiny tangerines, only tart. They make a superb marmalade. When I migrated north each May, I would pack jars of it in my station wagon to give to the generous friends who fed and bedded me along my route. I was always asked back. The wife of a ranger at Everglades National Park taught me to make it—Ida.

You have to halve and pit the globes (over a bowl to save the juice—they are mostly juice). That's the time-consuming part. Give peels and juice a very quick whirl in the blender, add 2 scant cups of water for every 1 cup of fruit (I skimp on this, there is so much juice). Simmer the mixture for 20 minutes, measure it, add an equal amount of sugar, and cook until it sheets. Like jelly.

TOMATO BUTTER

When you or your generous friends have more tomatoes than can be dealt with, cut up 7 pounds, leaving the peels on. Add 3 pounds of brown sugar, 1 tablespoon each of cinnamon and cloves, and 8 ounces of vinegar. Bring this to a boil, reduce the heat, and simmer for at least 2½ to 3 hours. Store the butter in a cool place, and eat fairly soon—it may mold.

TOMATO MARMALADE

This is from an old Long Island, New York, cookbook, handwritten at the turn of the century, when the Island grew potatoes, not lemons. I imagine the latter in those years were a considerable luxury, making this a special dish.

Set 4 pounds of ripe tomatoes briefly in boiling water so they will peel easily. Chop, add 6 lemons very thinly sliced, 1 cup of raisins, 4 pounds of sugar. Simmer these for 2 hours. "Sometimes this jells," the faded writing says, "sometimes not, but it is as good either way." Carol Flechner, an editor who sends me undeserved jars of marmalade and chutney out of her generous heart and redolent kitchen, suggests adding some finely minced crystallized ginger to this. She says it's terrific.

TOMATO CHUTNEY

Made the same way.

To 11 cups of peeled and chopped tomatoes (I don't know how many pounds that is; I just put in lots of tomatoes) add 2 garlic cloves, 1½ cups of sugar, 1 cup each of cider vinegar and raisins, 2 teaspoons of salt, ¼ to ½ teaspoon of red pepper or its equivalent, 2 teaspoons of ginger, 4 cinnamon sticks. Bring these to a boil, then simmer the mixture until it is thick—about 2 hours. Stir occasionally. The cinnamon sticks may be removed before filling your jars, but I often leave them in to impress my recipients.

Cranberries, Cranberries, Cranberries

Cranberry cakes, conserve, pancakes, sauces, jellies. Crimson tartness.

I am partial to cranberries. Full of vitamin C, they can be eaten as tart or sweet as you wish, keep well in fridge or freezer, cook quickly. Their juice is better for high blood pressure than martinis.

It's a tradeoff, though. I live in cranberry country. Walk down our dirt road one way, and you come out from under shading trees to a small crimson cranberry bog. The sky is wide above it, sunlit and azure in good weather, gray, with wind tugging low clouds across it, in bad; a wealth of stars and a crescent moon at night; or a full moon reflecting silver and gold between tree shadows. I look at its subtle, rich colors with mixed feelings. For years the cranberry market on Cape Cod was depressed. Small bogs were not economically viable, their edges grew up to dense shrubbery, where catbirds and yellow warblers nested, orioles called from slender locust branches above. Walk the other way, and there is a similar, older bog. For fifteen years, this has been increasingly ringed with impenetrable bushes, saplings, and pines. Its wet surface reflected the sunsets, the stars. It has been haven to spring peepers, to migrant birds, redwings and robins, flycatchers and thrush. Peaceful refuges for the spirit, both of these low openings. Now cranberries are profitable. This past year, the trees and shrubs have been torn out, replaced by piles of sand and burned tree trunks. Hoses block my path, flooding out what small vegetation remains. Wind still sweeps across space, stars still sparkle, but the wildflowers and birds are gone, the autumn harmony of autumn leaves. Children who venture there, hunting a few last wild cranberries, are chased away.

I try not to think of this as I buy cranberries at the market, listen to them pop in a saucepan on my stove. Hearing of this cookbook, my friends have pressed recipes upon me: cranberry bread, cranberry coffee cake, muffins, tarts, pies, puddings. Cranberries cooked and uncooked, with or without oranges, walnuts, apples. I've winnowed a few recipes for you—the easiest. If you want more, let me know. I can provide dozens.

CRANBERRY SAUCE, UNCOOKED

This is the easiest.

Break up 3 cups of cranberries briefly in a blender, or mash them by hand. Heat ½ cup each of sugar and currant jelly with ½ teaspoon of ground ginger, and add these to the berries. Mix, add grated orange and lemon peel, cover, and chill it for a day, or a week. Instead of ground ginger, chop up a few pieces of candied ginger. This adds a pleasant crunch.

If you don't want to wait a day, chop 2 cups of berries and 1 orange, add ¾ cup of sugar, stir the sauce, and let it sit for ½ hour. I add slivers of candied ginger to this, too.

CRANBERRY SAUCE, COOKED

Tart. Can be spiced with a stick of cinnamon and two or three whole cloves.

Cook over low heat 4 cups of berries in 2 cups of water until they are soft enough to be pressed through a strainer. Cook this over low heat, stirring, for 2 or 3 minutes, add 2 cups of sugar, a pinch of salt, and cook for a couple of minutes more. Chill.

You'll never eat store-bought cranberry sauce again.

SIMPLE CRANBERRY CONSERVE

Set 1 cup of raisins in ½ cup of boiling water to soften while you cook 4 cups of berries in ¾ cup of cold water until they pop. You can strain the berries or leave them whole. Grind an orange in a blender, using the raisin water to flush out any residue. Add orange and liquid to the berries with 1 cup of sugar. Cook this until it thickens, then add ½ cup of walnut meats and the raisins.

JO'S CRANBERRY CONSERVE

Jo Pettingill's recipe is more elaborate but worth the trouble. Jo is such a fine cook that if I had access to her recipe box, I wouldn't use anything else for this book. She's not a birder, but she is married to an eminent one, which ought to qualify her.

She chops 3 tangerines with 2 cups of cranberries and 1 peeled apple, adds ½ cup each of marmalade and vinegar, 1½ cups of water, 1¼ cups of sugar, ½ cup of raisins, ½ teaspoon each of ginger and cloves, ¼ teaspoon of cinnamon, 1 tablespoon of curry, a dash of allspice. (I don't know how she gets all this right.) She brings these to a boil and simmers them for 30 minutes, stirring them so they won't burn.

If you get to one of their Maine church suppers early enough, you might also be able to snaffle a jar of this from her.

CRANBERRY CATSUP

Jo puts this through a sieve—and I suppose if you are going to call it a catsup, you should, but I like it with the skins so I don't. Use a big kettle. For 4 pounds of berries (4 cups make 1 pound; halve the recipe, if you wish), she uses 1 pound of onions (that depends on their size—let your grocer do the weighing), chopped, 2 cups each of water and vinegar, 4 cups of sugar, 1 tablespoon of cloves, allspice, salt, cinnamon, and 1 teaspoon of black pepper. Cook the catsup until it is soft enough to sieve.

It's different. Thanks, Jo.

CRANBERRY CHUTNEY

Like Jo, Ginny Eckelberry is a gourmet cook. She is a fabric designer, not a birder; but being married to an eminent bird painter qualifies her. A shelf of cookbooks, ethnic and American, runs the length of their big carriage-house kitchen. She cooks always with a book propped before her, anxiously checking each spoonful and whisk. I can't tease her about this because everything she sets in front of us is so marvelous. This is her Cranberry Chutney.

To 1 package of cranberries (that's 3 cups) add 1½ cups of sugar, ½ teaspoon of allspice, ¼ teaspoon of salt, 1 teaspoon of cloves, 4 tablespoons of chopped orange rind plus 1 tablespoon of chopped lemon rind (whirl these briefly in the blender with 2 tablespoons of lemon juice and ½ cup of orange juice), 2 cups of raisins, 1 tablespoon of candied ginger. Let these stand for 10 minutes. Add 2 sticks of cinnamon, then simmer, covered, for another 30 minutes (longer, if it isn't thick enough—but keep an eye out for burning). Sliced almonds can be added at the end, if you want them. Wrapped attractively, in jelly glasses, you have a fine gift (for someone who doesn't live in cranberry country).

CRANBERRY CRUNCH FOR CORONARY CASES

This dessert has no eggs, a minimum of shortening, and can be served without the ice cream. Quick and easy.

You *can* use slices of cranberry sauce out of a can, but it's little trouble to put 1 cup of sugar, ½ cup of water on the stove with 2 cups of fresh cranberries, which will have popped by the time you have greased an oven-proof serving dish and mixed 1 cup each of brown sugar and rolled oats with ½ cup flour. Cut in ⅓ cup of shortening. A small wire whisk works well for this. When it is crumbly, spread half of it in your greased casserole, cover this with the cranberry sauce, cover this with the rest of the dry mixture, and let the Crunch bake at 350° for about 40 minutes while you and your guests are eating dinner. Don't let it overcook, and serve it warm with vanilla ice cream.

BETSY'S CRANBERRY CAKE

No butter. The cranberries cook in the baking.

Sprinkle ½ cup of sugar over 2 cups of cranberries that have been put in an oven-proof dish. Beat well 2 eggs with 1 cup of sugar; add 1 cup of flour, ½ cup of melted shortening, and pour this over the berries. Walnuts are optional. Bake at 325° for about 1 hour.

CRANBERRY PANCAKES

My friend Harriet lives on a hill above an ancestral bog, its bronze-red carpet lovely in autumn. "I hate cranberries," she exploded the other day, handing me a jar of her conserve. "I bake cranberry bread until my friends wince to see me coming, jars of cranberry-apple sauce fill our cold pantry. (Quite good, actually—I'll bring you some.) Last weekend, with all those young wedding guests staying with me, I even made Cranberry Pancakes. They turned out surprisingly well."

She had sprinkled cranberries with sugar and water, cooked them for a few minutes, then added them to 4 beaten eggs, 1 cup of yogurt, 2 tablespoons of baking powder, 1 tablespoon of sugar, 1¼ cups of flour, and a shake of salt.

"The batter was a bit thick, so we thinned the yogurt with milk. When the second batch was gone, one of the girls took over. She found cottage cheese in the fridge, used that instead of yogurt with enough milk to thin it, and substituted one-half cup of whole-wheat flour for white. She wanted buckwheat, but I didn't have any. They weren't bad, but you're pretty desperate when you put cranberries in *pancakes!*"

How did I get into all these? Americans eat too many sweets—I don't need to promote sugars. I suppose next you'll be wanting brownies and fudge and real cream in your coffee.

Salads

Salads run a gamut from just fesh greens with a really good oil-and-vinegar-and-herb dressing to the multitude that are meals in themselves. I can't deal with them. Not in a book, anyway. I love to eat them. I'd rather live on peasant soups and salads and an occasional roast chicken than most of the foods in this book. (Don't tell my editor.)

If I am feeding a group of any size, I stick pretty much to one of the following.

TOSSED SALAD

For color, to accompany a main dish, greens tossed with celery, onions, tomatoes, green peppers, carrot coins, Jerusalem artichokes (if I have any), and a tart dressing of oil, vine-gar, and herbs. If it is a big bowlful and no one is looking, I also mix in a raw egg.

POTATO SALAD

Potato salad means a lot of potatoes, boiled and peeled ahead. This salad needs to be done a day before anyway, so they can mellow with a generous amount of mayonnaise—preferably my mayonnaise, but any good one will do—onion, and season-ing. It can be a main meal with deviled eggs, cucumbers, and tomatoes edging it, green peas scattered on top; or it can accompany a buffet of cold, sliced meat. If any is left over, it is equally good the next day.

BULGUR SALAD

Also a main meal.

Pour twice as much boiling broth—chicken, vegetable, beef—or just plain water over the measure of bulgur, and let this stand, covered, until the liquid is absorbed. When it is cold, add mushrooms and vegetables, or raisins and carrots and a bit of chopped apple, or seafood, or chicken and celery—whatever. It should be served cold. It adapts nicely to being packed in cups to carry on a trip.

When we were living (briefly) in Paris, my husband had an assistant invaluable in introducing us to Gallic ways. I suspect she had a slight mash on him, but she was aware that I did, too, and respected this. Learning that restaurant meals were palling on us, one night she invited us for a light supper in her apartment. I was overjoyed. It turned out to be my kind of meal—a large round mound of bulgur full of mushrooms, with herbs, carrots, onions set on watercress. Moistened with lemon juice and sour cream, skirted with cucumber and tomato wedges. It looked lovely—she was an artist. What she didn't know (she hadn't thought to inquire) was that never in all the years I knew him was my man willing to eat—or even taste—any vegetable but beets (ironically, I disliked beets!). He was a meat-and-potatoes-and-pie man. The evening would have been a disaster then and there if the two of them hadn't been so charmingly amused. Cheese—there is always cheese—and bread. And wine. And affection. Nina her name was. Wherever she may be, I wish her well.

BEAN SALAD

Delis, supermarkets, and roadside fast-food stops offer this, and with good reason. It is nourishing and popular, the combinations plentiful. We used to call it Seven-Bean Salad, but I'm not sure what they all were. I use garbanzos, red kidney beans, black beans sometimes, both green and yellow beans, limas. I guess if black-eyed peas were added, you would be inching up on seven. I am well satisfied with only some of these, with sprouts, watercress (if it is available), with red and green peppers, onions, garlic, celery, parsley, marjoram or oregano, a dressing with chili sauce in it. Since tomatoes always add, even if only harmonious color, wedges of them can be set around the edges of the big bowl. This is more difficult in a cup!

FAMILY FESTIVE FOURTH OF JULY SEAFOOD SALAD

My doctor is a skinny fellow, in spite of his liking to eat. A good cook. Since I am always complaining to him that I weigh too much, he was amused to learn that I was writing a cookbook and needed to test—on him—some of the recipes I'm given so I won't get sued. (Doctors are very conscious of being sued.) He offered me his Salad, claiming it would feed 8 normal people or 12 dieters plus 3 children. As I looked at the ingredients, he responded to my critical eyebrows, saying canned shrimp and crab meat can be substituted for fresh, and the lobster skipped altogether. Maybe he could get away with that, but I surely wouldn't be able to—not unless I had led my participants into a fish store and let them gape at the prices of seafood these days.

He marinates 1 pound of pasta, cooked firm, with ¾ cup of oil, ¼ cup of malt vinegar, ⅓ cup of catsup, 1 teaspoon each of salt, pepper, and onion juice, and 2 tablespoons of lemon juice. This sits overnight in the fridge. Next day, he adds 3 stalks of celery and 1 medium onion, chopped fine, then ½ pound each of crab meat, cooked shrimp, and cooked lobster, 1 tablespoon of tarragon vinegar, ¼ cup of chopped parsley, ⅔ cup of mayonnaise, and ½ teaspoon of paprika.

I offered to provide the tarragon vinegar and mayonnaise, made by my loving hands, if he would arrange for the seafood, but he didn't pay attention—his telephone was ringing.

So on this bowl of glory, with firecrackers snapping, rockets bursting over a summer beach, children running between adults and waving sparklers, I will abandon salads. Just be sure that whatever dressing you anoint them with is *good;* and if you set the bottle on your table or picnic cloth, use an attractive one.

Desserts

NOODLE KUGEL

Let's get Noodle Kugel over with first. It was fed me—and, fortunately, several others—by a well-padded woman from Iowa after a bird lecture I had given. I still don't know whether it was a pasta dish or a dessert; but after eating my share, this didn't matter.

Cook 1 pound of wide noodles. Add ½ pound of butter, 4 ounces of cream cheese, 2 cups of milk, 2 cups of apricot nectar (that's what she said), ½ cup of golden raisins, 6 beaten eggs, ½ cup of sugar, a pinch of salt. Mix these well, pour them into a buttered dish, sprinkle with sugar and cinnamon, and bake at 350° for 45 to 60 minutes.

It's different (that's for sure) and feeds a group amply.

Pies

PECAN PIE

The first year I drove to Florida, all my goods and chattels and birdbanding equipment in my station wagon, to live in

unknown territory, in an uncertain future, I had been urged to stop at the Savannah River National Wildlife Refuge and convey greetings to the then-manager Pres Lane and his wife. The road I was on took me through their watery wilderness, embarrassingly about lunchtime, although I parked and walked wherever I could find paths in order to delay a little. The Lanes took me in, pressed a full second-day Thanksgiving dinner of turkey hash and pecan pie on me, gave me a royal tour of the acres of waterfowl they guarded. Turkey hash I am an old hand at. But pecan country was new to me, and the pie. They sent me off with a generous slice. It couldn't be simpler.

Mix 1 cup each of sugar, corn syrup, butter, broken pecans. Add 3 eggs, 1 tablespoon of flour, salt, vanilla. Put this into an unbaked pie crust, and bake at 325° until it is brown. It couldn't be better.

GIL'S BLUEBERRY PIE

Gil Fernandez is the kind of birder that is called a professional amateur. This means that while he has no degrees in ornithology, his contributions equal and often excel those of men who do. Twenty years ago, when successfully breeding ospreys had almost disappeared from New England, he learned that in Chesapeake Bay the U.S. Coast Guard was destroying osprey nests. The big fish hawks were building their bulky homes on buoy lights, rendering these ineffective to navigation. Gil went to Maryland and brought back eggs from the nests (on buoy lights) of the healthy birds there to be fostered in the only five remaining active nests he knew of on his neighboring Westport River in Massachusetts. He had to invent a safe carryall for the eggs. He had to enlist the help of the Coast Guard in getting him up to the nests in their watery habitat. He had to persuade them that there must be a better way to safeguard their buoys than destroying birds as valuable—and scenic—as ospreys. For years, he climbed to nests, guarded, photographed, protectively publicized them. In his seventies, he is still setting out nest poles on the East and West Branches of the river, supervising these, keeping careful records of successes and failures. He lectures, with fine and historical photographs, out of his philosophy that all of God's creatures are interconnected, dependent upon each other. Now, on the Westport River alone, he can count fifty nests active, with some adults producing clutches of four eggs where three is the usual number. There is an amateur for you!

He used to be a restaurateur. I first knew him as a small, modest man who, with his wife Jo, drove a considerable distance twice a week to volunteer as birdbander at the Manomet Bird Observatory in its early years. They would bring baskets of food for the hungry crew, of which I was one. Everything was good, but the best was Gil's Blueberry Pie.

"Fill a baked pie shell," he says, shrugging. "It's no problem." But the fine, flaky crust he makes is not what comes out of *my* kitchen, nor most of those I know. "Cook one cup of blueberries with one cup of sugar and three heaping tablespoons of cornstarch until thickened. Add berries to fill the shell—you'll use probably four cups in all. Give a quick squeeze of lemon. When the filling is cool, top with cream cheese mixed to a good consistency with sour cream, and dust with cinnamon. If I use a really big pie tin, as I do for you all, it takes another cup of berries but I don't change the base. I mix the topping until I think I have enough. Or add more, if I don't."

All I can say is, there are cooks and cooks. And amateur professionals. Not many like Gil.

PUMPKIN PIE

I make pumpkin pie because (1) I like it; (2) there are those pumpkins and squash at my front door, waiting to be used (or, if I'm lazy, all I need to do is open a can of pumpkin or squash, which is equally good—the spices effectively control the taste; besides, I always flavor my mixture with a table-spoonful of rum); and (3) it transports more easily than lemon meringue or chocolate. (I once tripped and dropped a chocolate pie bringing it into my mother-in-law's dining room. The catastrophe scarred me.)

I read the recipes in books and in my file box for Pumpkin Pie. Some use 2 eggs, some 3 (which make a slightly larger pie). Some use 1½ cups of pumpkin, some 2 cups (ditto). They all seem to list 1½ cups of milk, which can be evapo-rated or whole. The sugar varies from ½ to 1 full cup and can be both white and brown, mixed. Cloves and ginger are ½ teaspoon each, cinnamon and ginger can vary—up to 1½ tea-spoons. Some cooks add 1 spoonful of molasses, and I use rum. When I am tired of studying up on these, I pretty much make up my own. Three beaten eggs added to 1½ to 2 cups of pumpkin or squash, 1½ cups of evaporated milk (if I happen to have any) or regular milk, the spices as above, with a liberal hand with ginger. I mix all these with cheerful disregard for nit-picking instructions, pour the result into a pie shell of my own concocting—sometimes a conventional crust, sometimes one made of cinnamon crackers rolled fine and blended into melted butter—and bake it. The recipes tell me to start with a hot oven, 425°, and after 10 or 15 minutes turn this down to 325° or 300°. The minutes and the temperature vary, as do I, busy doing something else. It takes about ¾ hour to bake the pie, depending on how many eggs and how much rum I may have used. So I slide a knife into its center when I start to get nervous or if the crust browns too rapidly to please me.

I cool my product and then, before carrying it to whatever destination, ornament it with sweetened whipped cream liberally flavored with rum or bourbon. If there are young people, I use lots of whipped cream, thickly spread. For their more diet-conscious elders, I drop on half a dozen dollops of the cream, artfully concealing the cuts my knife has made.

It's a versatile dish, tidy, easy to cut. No need to worry about leftovers. (Fanny Farmer has a terrific recipe for Parsnip Pie—that's next on my agenda. I incorporate honey, lemon juice, orange rind. I could offer a prize to whoever guesses its base.)

APPLE PIE

The standard pie for dessert or breakfast, for a midday snack, if you are really hungry, is Apple. To satisfy my family, I had to learn to cope with Lemon Meringue or Key Lime, which means a lot of stirring, a careful eye on cooking both crust and meringue. So I stick with Apple when I can. If the crust isn't the best (as I said, there are cooks and cooks), you don't have

to eat it—blue jays will be glad to. If *I* am making it—well, of course it's good—even jays like it. If you haven't time to make a top crust, you can omit it. I have one friend who omits the bottom crust, too. She says all people really want is the apples, tart with lemon, sweet with sugar.

Frances Hamerstrom, on page 123 of her marvelously funny book *Birding with a Purpose* (Ames: Iowa State University Press, 1984), tells of eating an excellent one on the Mackenzie Highway: "Just slice the apples, put them in the sun, and leave 'em until you can still bend the pieces. They'll turn brown, so you put in a little extra cinnamon to disguise the color," their sourdough host told them. It is gray and rainy a lot on Cape Cod; I've not been successful in drying apples. Maybe, I console myself, when you are driving the Mackenzie Highway, hunting a nonexistent gas station, an apple pie of any sort is delectable. (When they could no longer find road-killed rabbits, Dr. Hamerstrom also recommended "porcupine fried with onions and bacon, with hot pepper added. Served with beans. Delicious." I no longer live in porcupine country, but I've filed this recipe in the back of my mind—I'd like to try it. I liked raccoon and possum and hand-raised rabbit the lucky times I was offered these in the South, so why not porcupine? Frequently here, I pass road-killed rabbits and squirrels, and, as I slide these into the plastic bag I carry for this purpose, I weigh whether to take them home to cook or whether to deliver them to a rehabilitation station that always has owls and hawks in need of natural dinners. So far, since my finds would have to be skinned, the owls have won.)

I came across "Philip Wylie's Apple Pie" in an elegant cookbook by Frany Fury (Providence, R.I.: Providence Athenaeum, 1981). We had dinner once with Philip Wylie at the even more elegant Plaza-Athénée in Paris, ending up with wild strawberries and *lots* of wine. To me he was an impressive character from the World of Letters (just minor, he assured my shyness). To my husband he was simply an old college friend fortuitously encountered. Finding his name and pie brought back many memories of our tours of duty in Paris and the restaurants we tried, settling finally on a cosy Italian one around the corner from our hotel, where the owner's collie made friends, assessed us for largesse, curled up at our feet under our wooden table with its peasant cloth. Around the walls, a frieze of wine bottles (empty) reflected the light, as did our wine goblets (full). The food was simple and excellent. But after the Duke and Duchess of Windsor discovered and adopted it, the dog was banished, the owners attempted to become sophisticated, we had to abandon it.

The inclusion of Philip by the Athenaeum was a tribute, I fear, to his literary reputation rather than to his culinary taste. The recipe offered nothing but thinly sliced apples (only one layer at that) arranged on crust, sprinkled with sugar, dotted with butter, and baked. No grated lemon peel or juice, no ginger, no cinnamon, no obligatory sharp Vermont cheese served with it. He doesn't even warn that the apples you use are important: some kinds bake down to sauce, some hold their shape permanently, some soften to delectable forkfuls. I use lots of apples—the green Granny Smiths, sweet but firm; I have a friend who swears by Gravensteins. We both layer these on a mix of 1 cup of sugar and 1 tablespoon of flour, use lots of lemon, cinnamon, top with more mix, sprinkle with lemon juice, grated lemon, and cinnamon, dot well with butter. This can have a top crust or be baked as is. I tried it once (I had been reading a magazine at the hairdresser's) with the cheese mixed into the apples and a spoonful of molasses dropped onto it. I didn't like it.

"Why not maple syrup instead of the molasses?" asked a Vermont daughter-in-law, gathering up my apple peels to stew with a little water and sugar and lemon-peel strips. "To make a syrup for baked or stewed apples, or to put in herb tea," she answered my inquiring look. Vermonters waste nothing—they get snowed in too often. "Or for apple pancakes," she added. She has a small apple orchard.

Crisps

MAJOR'S APPLE CRISP

While we are on the subject of apples, here is Major's Apple Crisp, from the Adirondacks.

Dice 2 apples. Beat well 1½ cups of brown sugar and 2

eggs, stir in 3 tablespoons of flour, 1½ teaspoons of baking powder, 2 teaspoons of cinnamon, ½ teaspoon of nutmeg, a pinch of salt, ½ cup of raisins, ½ cup of walnut meats. Mix this with the apples, and bake in a heavily buttered, fairly deep pan. Serve it with ice cream or whipped cream while it is warm (but not to dieters).

APPLE, RHUBARB, OR PEACH CRISP

"Cooks are always trying to improve things instead of leaving them alone," an Air Force officer grumped at me when I served him a bowl of applesauce with slivered lemon rind, almonds, and candied ginger in it. "Why don't we just eat apples as God made them?" I noticed, though, that he emptied his bowl, and not entirely out of good manners. I didn't offer him any one of these crisps.

These are seasonal dishes. To apples, I add golden raisins; to rhubarb, strawberries, fresh or frozen; peaches I let stand by themselves with grated lemon and juice. For rhubarb, use 1 cup less fruit.

For the apple crisp, put 5 cups of fruit (that's maybe 8 apples, peeled) into a greased baking dish. (If you can't get good, tart apples, don't even try this dessert.) Over these, put a topping made from ½ cup of flour, ⅓ cup of rolled oats, ¾ cup of brown sugar, ⅓ cup of butter, 1 teaspoon of cinnamon, ½ teaspoon of salt. Work this lightly, as you would pastry. Bake the crisp at 350° for about 30 minutes (depending upon how deep your dish is) or until the apples are tender. Serve plain or with cream or vanilla ice cream. This should yield 6 portions.

Fruit

QUICK-AND-EASY MAJOR'S BAKED PEACHES

Cook down the syrup from a can of peaches to which has been added a dollop of butter and grated lemon rind. Pour this over the fruit, and heat in a slow oven while your guests eat the main course. Add a splash of brandy or rum before serving—with ice cream, if you want. The more people eating, the more cans of peaches and lemon rind. Slivered candied ginger is good in this, too. You can use Bing cherries instead of peaches. These *should* be served with ice cream.

BETS EDWARD'S PICKLED FRUIT

This is healthier than the baked peaches. It doesn't taste pickled.

Simmer for 10 minutes 1 cup of sugar, ¼ cup of vinegar, 1 stick of cinnamon, 1 teaspoon of whole cloves, and ½ cup of liquid from 3 cups of drained canned peaches or pears or cherries or apricots or pineapple (or a mixture of these). Add the fruit, heat it through slowly, cover it with extra juice, and let it stand 24 hours. Cool and chill. Before serving, splash with white wine or rosé.

Gingerbread

"You *have* to put in your Gingerbread," a granddaughter wrote me from West Germany. (I had her researching Black Bread.) "You know the most reason I come to see you is your gingerbread. It makes me homesick just to think about it. Even when I couldn't have it with whipped cream [she is a ballet dancer]. If it's in a book, I can still have the recipe when you die, your file cards will get lost. It's better than Corn Bread, and *much* more nourishing than cake."

I don't think I have any trick with gingerbread. I use more ginger than the recipes call for; I am careful *not* to let it cook that last 5 minutes the instructions call for, so it is moist and chewy (although sometimes it is *too* moist—the line is fine). I use recipes that call for yogurt or buttermilk when I have those to get rid of. But what I mostly stick with is Alice's Gingerbread.

ALICE'S GINGERBREAD

Combine ½ cup of shortening with 1 cup of brown sugar, 2 eggs, 2 cups of flour, 1 teaspoon each of soda and nutmeg, ½ teaspoon of salt, 2 teaspoons of ginger, and ½ cup of boiling water with ½ cup of molasses in it. Lots of raisins. Bake at 350°. How long? I'm not sure—40 minutes? If it's dry, I don't like it. I can get around that by putting ½ cup of applesauce into it—*my* applesauce, unstrained, lumpy, not store-bought applesauce. Or, for a real dessert, not something to pack to take on a bird trip, I pour the batter over sliced peaches in the baking pan.

Some Cakes

MOLLY'S CARROT CAKE

I was going to put Cakes in the cookie section. But since we are into Alice's Gingerbread, I might as well give you her cousin Molly's recipe for carrot cake.

To ¾ cup of butter creamed with ¼ cup of sugar, add 3 beaten eggs, 1½ teaspoons of baking powder, 2 cups of flour, ¼ teaspoon of salt, ½ cup each of grated carrots and chopped almonds. Bake the cake at 325° for 1 hour, then pour over it ⅓ cup of orange juice heated just enough to dissolve ½ cup of sugar. Serves 12. (Don't forget the eggs. I did once, disastrously, though I later redeemed it with a custard sauce poured over it.)

AMANDA'S BUTTERMILK CAKE

Molly is a much better cook than I am, and so is her Aunt Amanda, who turns out with barely a flick of her wrist a fine Buttermilk Cake. It is baked in a big pan at 375° for 30 minutes. No eggs.

She mixes ½ cup of oil with 1 cup of sugar, 1 cup of buttermilk or sour milk, 1½ teaspoons of vanilla, then adds 1⅔ cups of flour, ½ cup of cocoa, 1 teaspoon of baking soda, ½ teaspoon of salt. It's not rich and has crispy edges.

More Desserts

What I was really looking for back a good many pages was black bread, not cakes! But since we are now into Desserts, let's continue.

PEARS

My grandmother had a pear tree in her back garden. One of my childhood memories is of standing on tiptoe in the hot summer sun, trying to reach those pears hanging just out of reach—golden, sun-warmed, delicious. Many years later in Buffalo, I planted a dwarf Bartlett in our small back yard. Its fruit bowed the branches to the ground; it was the delight of all small children on the block. The children and I liked the pears raw, but for my husband I would peel and cook them in a sugar syrup made with slivered lemon peel and a few pieces of candied ginger. Half a cup of sugar to 1 cup of water. If your tooth is sweeter, use more sugar. I would stew the pears gently until they were tender but still firm. For company, I would remove the pears, cook the syrup down almost to the thickness of honey, add a spoonful of liqueur to it, and pour this over the fruit.

I tried making my own liqueurs from peaches or apricots, adding vodka to these, letting them sit in the dark, covered tightly, but even after six weeks these tasted more of alcohol than of fruit (or not of alcohol at all), and failed to produce the deep golden color I was hoping for. I have a neighbor who assured me she was successful making beach-plum liqueur. Her result was a fine deep crimson, lovely to hold up to the light; but, alas, it tasted (to me, anyway) like the thick red cough syrup I was forced to gag on as a child. It's important to get along with neighbors, so I expressed admiration of her effort but quickly disposed of any recipe she pressed on me. Tastes differ. You may not like *any* of my recipes. I won't hold it against you.

Pears—that's what we were discussing. In France, where they are delicious, as a treat we were expensively served them one night coated with chocolate sauce, which shocked and outraged our taste buds. Poires Hélène I think they called them. A simpler addition would be a spoonful of Cointreau or red wine and lemon, but what is wrong with just that trace of ginger and lemon in the syrup?

If you really want to fancy pears up, you can add 1 can of strained cranberry sauce to 1 cup of pear syrup, cook this gently for 15 minutes, pour the sauce over the halved pears, and bake these at 350° for another 15 minutes, basting from time to time. Set the pears on a warm platter, spoon the glaze over them, put a spoonful of brandy in each hollow, and ignite. Only by the time I get the last one lit the first one is out. It's less formal but more fun to try this at the table. (It doesn't always work, but lots of things in life don't work—you just keep laughing.)

BANANAS

You can flambé bananas, too, by cutting them lengthwise and cooking them in a thickened syrup of 4 tablespoons of butter, ¾ cup of brown sugar, and cinnamon until they are soft. Add rum and a little Crème de Banane (if you can find it), and ignite.

Both flambéed pears and bananas demand an attractive, oven-proof dish that can be brought to the table.

WINE JELLY

I am just a simple birdwatcher with simple tastes. I prefer my fruits uncooked and my flames from candles. Let's shift to the delicate colors and taste of wine jelly.

When our Number 1 son lay stricken in a Veterans Hospital with pneumonia one long-ago March, an elderly friend of ours, distressed, took him a bowl of pale-green Wine Jelly to celebrate Saint Patrick's Day. She was ignorant of the chemical reaction of alcohol combined with drugs. The jelly was cool, delicious. Our son licked up every spoonful—and paid the price. So be sure of your guests' medical condition.

She softened 2½ tablespoons of gelatin in ½ cup of cold water, then dissolved this in 1½ cups of boiling water, adding 1 cup of sugar and stirring to dissolve this, too. When it had cooled, she added ½ cup of sherry, 3 tablespoons of brandy, 6 tablespoons of Kirsch, ⅓ cup of orange juice, 3 tablespoons of lemon juice. If it is Saint Valentine's Day or Christmas, use red coloring, she said. Green for Saint Patrick's. It slides down, as our son can testify, very easily. And up . . .

Memories

I'm not a gourmet. I remember special dishes—some of them are in this book—because of where and with whom I ate them. Shrimp sandwiches in a small dock restaurant after a langorous morning on Florida Bay with two men with whom I enjoyed contemplating herons and spoonbills, ibis, the low-flapping pelican that nested in white-splashed mangroves. Trifle in Trinidad long before Asa Wright's Spring Hill Estate had become a nature center—when rats nibbled on the teacakes she kept shut up in an armoire, vampire bats nibbled on her donkey. Visiting birders in her good graces, residents like myself, were offered that Trifle from a bowl that held at least four kinds of cake and surely as many "spirits," so that afterward, when you saw tanagers and honey creepers at her feeders, you didn't know whether their bright colors were real or products of her "high teas." On Tobago, where I could count eight motmots before I had lifted my head from my pillow at Eleanor Alefounder's, I can still tell you what we ate for breakfast and what the thrush hopping on her kitchen counter as I prepared our eggs was eating for breakfast, too. Roast wapiti, venison, pigeon, the crimson jams and golden sherry on our tables in Geneva, in Barcleona, in Ceylon, now become Sri Lanka (where is Ceylon these days, with elephants raising their trunks as our car eased by them on the roadsides?)—all have surroundings as important to me as my memories of their tastes.

And More Desserts

GRACE'S FROZEN BRANDY-ALEXANDER PIE

A dozen of us or more (people came and went—it was hard to keep track) were sleeping at a Colorado ranch during an Audubon Conference. Couches, cots, mattresses, sleeping bags were pressed into service for members of the Sanctuary and Research Departments and what wives, knowing the kitchen duties they must cope with, were willing to come. It was marvelous—a cold wind without; a roaring fire, fine talk, fine food, fine liquor, the most congenial of company within. I suppose I took the hams and turkey and salads of the final dinner for granted—what else could you serve such a hearty crew? It is the dessert I clearly remember, perhaps because eventually I was the one who mopped the floor. We had started dessert with Frozen Brandy-Alexander Pies that Grace had made well ahead and had stashed in her freezer. They were so good the supply ran out. Never phased by feeding people, Grace pulled out quarts of vanilla ice cream, her blender, and started mixing 2 shots of brandy, 2 shots of Crème de Cacao to 1 quart of ice cream. "That's for four, but sometimes," she understated, "you need more ice cream." The kitchen became awash as "measurements for four" were ladled again and again into the blender. Years later, with a group of conference birders about to use *my* couches and cots and sleeping bags, I telephoned Colorado to ask what that dessert had been, how I should make it. Grace didn't hesitate, she knew immediately what—and when— I referred to. So if you have a dozen hearty outdoorsmen counting on you to recoup their energies and they bring lady friends willing to wash and mop and wipe, you can try her Pie. Perhaps if you can put enough pies in your freezer, you won't have to mess up the kitchen with all that ice cream. You could send her a post card, via me, thanking her. She would enjoy that.

For 1 9-inch pie, combine 1 14-ounce can of Eagle Brand condensed milk, 1 cup of whipping cream, 2 tablespoons each of brandy and Crème de Cacao. Pour this into a prebaked crust, and freeze it. Garnish the pie with shaved chocolate. "Return any leftovers to the freezer," she said, but I pointed out that that was a fantasy. Figure out your own interpretation of her "shot." It's not a bartender's 1 ounce.

BRANDY ALEXANDER

Supplement Grace's pie, as needed, with the following.

Blend 2 shots (see above) each of brandy and Crème de Cacao. No garnish needed. Serve this over vanilla ice cream before it turns to mush. Yields 4 portions. I've tried this using coffee ice cream, Amaretto, and brandy. It is equally good (as doubtless it would be with other substitutions), but it didn't bring back the same memories.

Grace says the recipes came to her from a woman named Loveless. I can't believe it. That Pie attracted men like honeybees.

DIPLOMAT'S DELIGHT

This equally rich concoction will send you back to apples and rhubarb or plain black coffee. It was taught me by a ranking government wife who had just returned from Thailand.

Her advice to me when she learned I was about to become a Government Wife of Status was to buy lots of dinner dresses and elbow-length gloves. I don't think she had ever heard of birdwatchers or, maybe, even apples. It's a terrific dessert, though. Very rich. Feeds 12.

Line 2 bread pans with crushed vanilla wafers or cinnamon crisps (better), saving some for the topping. About 20 will be enough.

Soften 1 17-ounce bar of Hershey's Almond Chocolate in the top of a double boiler, cool it slightly, add 1 pint of heavy cream, whipped. Set this in the pans, sprinkle each with a topping of crushed wafers, chill the desserts overnight, serve them with a dab of whipped cream sprinkled with crushed peppermint candy. (I crush these by banging them with a hammer in a bag of some sort—it's the hardest part.)

CHOCOLATE MOUSSE

An alternative to Diplomat's Delight, if you insist on killing your friends with calories, is this Chocolate Mousse, made by melting in a double boiler the Hershey bar in ¼ cup of hot coffee, adding 8 egg yolks, and cooking this until it coats a metal spoon. When the mixture is cool, add 8 beaten egg whites. Chill overnight, and serve it, too, with a dab of whipped cream. If you want peppermint flavor, you can melt chocolate peppermints with the Hershey bar.

ICE CREAM PLUS

As effective and no work at all is coffee ice cream (or vanilla) with almond slivers and a couple of spoonfuls of Amaretto.

DULCE DE QUESO

I started this Dessert section with a pasta, so here is a fitting coda from Colombia.

Thinly slice 1 pound of mozzarella, and arrange these in a baking dish. Bring 1 cup of water, 2 cups of brown sugar, a stick (or shake) of cinnamon to boiling, stir to dissolve the sugar, then cook slowly for 5 minutes. Pour this over the cheese, and serve immediately although it can be set in a preheated oven for a few minutes. Simple.

My real advice on desserts is to serve a bowl of fresh fruit, uncooked, unsweetened. It can be garnished with sprigs of green and flowers, and offered with fruit knives.

Cookies

I keep pushing the subject of cookies to one side. But if I neglect them, someone will show up at bird meetings and trips with store-bought cookies—a thought that makes me suffer. There *are* good store cookies that, like doughnuts, take an edge off your hunger, but they belong in a category by themselves.

Chocolate-chip cookies, brownies, hermits—books and store packages instruct on these (some recipes I've purloined). Mine have to be quick and easy to please me—and make *enough*. If they rarely turn out the same twice, what does that matter? Unless they are burned—and sometimes even that doesn't matter. I substitute, use what's handy. As—

OVERNIGHT MACAROONS

Last week I had a group of twenty college students come to me for a seminar on birds and a demonstration of birdbanding. I net songbirds (under license from the federal and state governments); record their age, sex, parasites, molt, general condition, weight; release them with a lightweight metal numbered government band on their legs so that, with luck, their migra-

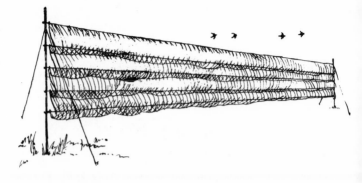

tions and longevity may be traced; add to the bits and pieces of ornithological knowledge being developed so that, again, with luck, species may be saved from the Endangered List. I didn't expect these students; they gave me only an hour's warning.

"But it's *raining*," I wailed. "I can't catch birds in the rain. *I* don't mind getting wet, but they get too tangled in the nets, their feathers come off in my hands. Birds need their feathers. I won't be able to do anything for you but talk."

That didn't put them off, just me. They had an empty, rainy afternoon to fill. Cookies, I thought. They'll be hungry, these will distract them. I had a recipe I wanted to try. Overnight Macaroons. The directions said to let the base sit for 8 hours, but I ignored that. Not having enough molasses, I eked out with brown sugar. I added wheat germ (young people need nourishment as well as sweets), substituted 1 cup of whole-wheat flour for white, cut up figs—they would make the result chewier. I was low on eggs or I would have added a second— I think this recipe needs it. No almond extract on my shelves, but there was Amaretto in a cupboard. The first batch came out well—I was in the kitchen, watching, while I filled the second pan. A bit tough, though, I thought, sampling. Needed that second egg. Later, when I wanted to check on this, I couldn't—they were all gone. All gone? My victims came up the path as I put the third pan in the oven. By the time they were sorted about my room, smoke and smell in the kitchen reminded us that I was cook as well as teacher. We pulled the smoking pan out, opened doors and windows.

"Here," I ordered one girl, distractedly. "Throw these out that far door for the birds. Maybe they will bring in jays for you to look at." She took pot holder and pan from me, started across the living room. Before she achieved the door, reaching hands had blocked her way, the pan was empty. Kids! I love them. Any age.

All right, I thought a week later, I'll make those again. I really want to know. With two eggs. Let the base sit overnight. Only in the midst of my measuring, I was interrupted, had to go out. Next day, a bowl of molasses, brown sugar, and oats leered at me. My interruption had been traumatic, the file card had disappeared. What had I been making? Why? I scraped the mess into a big jar and set it in my fridge until I might remember. (Nothing there to spoil. My motto, as I've said is: Waste Nothing.) A week later, when life had resumed a normal pace, I remembered. Expedition Seminar Cookies. Only where was the recipe? A week after that, I was typing a draft of this manuscript and—Eureka!—came upon a page which read: "Overnight Macaroons—practically instant."

One cup of oil, it read, poured over 2 cups of brown sugar and 4 cups of quick oats. Let this sit for 8 hours. (That's too much oil—try ¾ cup.) Well, these weren't going to be "instant," but I would give it another try. I pulled my mystery jar from the fridge. That evening, the instructions continued, while you are getting dinner, mix in 1 egg, 1 teaspoon each of salt and almond extract (or Amaretto). Drop the dough from a teaspoon onto a well-greased baking sheet, bake at 325° for about 12 minutes. Remove the result PROMPTLY.

"You can start these the night before and cook them during breakfast," the woman who had told me about them said, "when your family and guests aren't as apt to pilfer." I still wasn't sure how many oats were in that jar in my fridge, but the cookies turned out okay. Use 2 eggs, not 1—

Actually, I think other people's food tastes so good because you don't have to plan, purchase, stir, bake, and clean up yourself. That's a lot of dividends.

MACAROONS

Another version. These really *are* instant, if you bake them on a very well-greased pan and take them off *as soon as they come out of the oven.*

Whip 2 egg whites to soft peaks. Drizzle in 1 cup of sugar, 1 teaspoon of vanilla, 1 cup of coconut, and ½ cup of chopped dates. (The dates are my idea—they add a good texture.) Bake at 300 to 325° for 12 minutes. (Ovens differ.)

CHRISTMAS CHEWS

These are healthier, but still a type of Macaroon. The coconut can be exchanged for raisins or chopped nuts or dates (and why not put in some coconut anyway?). If you use almonds, substitute ¾ teaspoon of almond extract (or, again, Amaretto) for the vanilla.

Stir ¼ cup of powdered milk into ⅔ cup of sweetened condensed milk. Add ¼ cup of wheat germ, a dash of salt, and 1½ cups of coconut or substitutes. Drop in spoonfuls onto well-oiled heavy brown paper that has been placed on a cookie sheet, and bake at 325° for 12 to 15 minutes. Remove them from the paper while they are still hot, or you will be sorry.

CARY'S BOURBON BALLS

"And what's wrong with figs or dates stuffed with cream cheese and nuts?" asked my dentist, drilling into teeth that grew up on ribbon candy and marshmallows. "Do you have to eat all that sugar?" He didn't complain, though, when I brought him Bourbon Balls left over from a Christmas party. They're a bit of a nuisance to make but keep splendidly in a tin and are an effective holiday gift.

Combine 3 cups of crushed crackers with 1 cup of crushed nuts, 1 cup of confectioners' sugar, ½ tablespoon of cocoa, 3 teaspoons of honey or Karo syrup, ½ cup of bourbon or rum. Chill the dough overnight. Then roll pieces of it into small balls, and roll these in confectioners' sugar. Store the balls in a tight tin for 5 days before using them.

BRUCE SORRIE'S OATMEAL MBO SPECIALS

Healthier by far.

Bruce used to make these at Manomet Bird Observatory. The kitchen was always busy with hungry interns. They ate my bread so fast that in self-defense I had to teach them to make their own, in between taking birds out of our mist nets. I don't know what they did for cookies when Bruce left—I never see cookies on their kitchen table. Probably eaten before they have cooled. Bruce was on the staff in various capacities for a period, then moved on in various directions—ever upward. I often wonder how many cheerful people have munched on this product. Certainly, I have fed it over the years to hundreds of clamorous birdwatchers and have given out his instructions as freely as he gave them to me.

Cream 1 cup of shortening with 2½ cups of sugar. Beat in 4 eggs, one at a time, ⅔ cup of molasses, 3½ cups of flour (I add ½ cup of wheat germ here), 2 teaspoons each of salt, baking soda, cinnamon, and nutmeg; stir in 4 cups of rolled oats; then add raisins, nuts, chocolate chips, coconut ad lib. (You don't need *all* of these, but the interns like them.) Bake the cookies on a greased sheet for 10 minutes at 400°. (Ovens vary; all cookies demand watching. My file card for these is so bethumbed, it is hard to read.)

SIX-DOZEN REFRIGERATOR CINNAMON COOKIES

When you haven't time to stir up Bruce's cookies, look in your freezer. If you are provident, perhaps you will find in the back somewhere, rolled in plastic, stored for emergencies, the dough to make these.

Cream 1 cup of shortening with 2 cups of sugar; add 2 eggs, 1 teaspoon of vanilla, 1 cup of rolled oats, 3 cups of flour, 1 teaspoon each of baking soda and cream of tartar, ½ teaspoon of salt, 1 or 2 cups of sliced almonds. Mix, chill, and shape the dough into rolls. Chill again for 5 to 6 hours. Slice into cookies, and dip the cookies into ½ cup of sugar mixed with 4 teaspoons of cinnamon. Bake at 350° for about 10 minutes.

This is basic. I vary it with brown or white sugar, substitute 1 cup of whole-wheat flour and a shake of wheat germ for some of the white flour, add coconut, depending on whether I am using the cookies for a "Ladies' Tea," children, or birdwatchers stopping in from a day in the field to tell me what they have seen while I lazily stayed home. The rolls can vary in size, too. I try to keep one in my freezer, always ready to slice and use in emergencies. If I lack time, I don't bother the dips in the cinnamon sugar I keep in a jar on a shelf.

OLD-FASHIONED SOUR-CREAM COOKIES

Another day, if I have sour cream left over from concocting cocktail-party dips, I make these.

Cream ½ cup of shortening with 1 cup of brown sugar. Beat in 2 eggs, 1 cup of sour cream, salt, ½ teaspoon each of baking soda and cinnamon, 2 teaspoons of baking powder, and 2 cups of flour. Vary by using light or dark sugar, whole-wheat flour, a bit of wheat germ, or oatmeal for some of the white flour.

These make 20 good-sized grandchildren cookies, many small party ones. They come out round and firm, so they can easily be iced and decorated for parties. If you have a light hand, you can draw a bird on a branch in the soft icing or make a pattern with nuts and candied cherry bits. This gives a festive touch. If you have a light hand.

SALLY RICHARDS'S UNBELIEVABLE PEANUT-BUTTER COOKIES

All these sweets are bad for us; we consume too much sugar. But cookies are mighty handy to eke out lunch, finish a dinner, quiet a children's car pool, and are invaluable to birders needing quick energy. So I will continue with a few more.

Some of them are healthier than others, like these peanut-butter cookies.

Mix thoroughly (an electric beater is most effective) 1 cup of creamy peanut butter with 1 egg, 1 cup of sugar, 1 teaspoon vanilla. Roll the dough with your hands into inch-sized balls, and place them on an ungreased cookie sheet about 1 inch apart. Bake in a preheated 300° oven for about 15 to 20 minutes. The yield of 24 cookies can vary with the size of the balls. They *are* unbelievable!

Sally lives 60 miles across an Arizona desert from the nearest supermarket, but her children had the normal appetite for cookies. How she happened to invent these I don't know, and it took me time to dare to try them. But they are great. At least she doesn't have to speak Spanish when she buys peanut butter.

LAC DES ABATIS BROWN-SUGAR CHEWY BROWNIES

When I lived 60 miles from market in Quebec, I had to deal in French-Canadian. I had three specials—all chewy. This is Number 1. They ride well in a pocket or fishing creel, but don't cook them too long if you want them chewy. I packed them when I would be gone all day in the woods, paddling a small canoe up little inlets, where warblers were thick in the leaves, where moose stopped eating water lilies to regard me, where the late raspberry bushes had bear trails wandering through them.

Cream ½ cup of shortening with 2 cups of brown sugar; add 2 eggs, 2 teaspoons of vanilla, 1 cup of flour, 2 teaspoons of baking powder, ½ teaspoon of salt, and nutmeats. Bake the brownies at 350° for 30 mintues, checking toward the end.

CHEWY MOLASSES COOKIES

Number 2.

Cream ¾ cup of shortening with 1 cup of brown sugar. Add 1 egg, 4 tablespoons of molasses, 2 teaspoons of baking soda, ¼ teaspoon each of salt and cloves, 1 teaspoon each of cinnamon and ginger (especially ginger). Drop by spoonfuls on a cookie sheet, sprinkle with sugar (or don't bother), and bake for 12 to 15 minutes at 375°. These also travel well in a pocket.

CHEWY WALNUT SQUARES

Number 3—for when we were low on shortening. (I don't really care for bacon grease in cookies!) No butter.

Mix 1 unbeaten egg with 1 cup of brown sugar, 1 teaspoon of vanilla, ½ cup of flour, ¼ teaspoon each of baking soda and salt. Add 1 cup of chopped walnuts. Spread this in a baking tin, and bake for 18 to 20 minutes at 350°. Cut it into squares.

SUPER MOLASSES COOKIES

I have feminist city friends who, looking over this manuscript for me, have complained that Males aren't adequately represented. So here is a cookie recipe from a Male. He must have been a Scout Master is all I can say. It makes 108 reasonably sized cookies, and he must have stayed up until midnight baking them. Still, I am grateful to him because even though I make only half the dough, I have found these cookies invaluable.

Mix the dough the night before—it should be allowed to sit.

Cream 1 cup of shortening with 1 cup of sugar. Add 2 cups of molasses, 1 egg, 2 teaspoons of vinegar, 4 scant teaspoons of baking soda dissolved in 1 cup of boiling water, then 5½ cups of flour—or ½ cup more, if you decide the dough is too thin. (I substitute 2 cups of whole-wheat flour for white.) Stir in 1 teaspoon of salt, 1 tablespoon of ginger, 1½ teaspoons of cinnamon, ¼ teaspoon of nutmeg, and ad lib with 1 cup of raisins and 1 cup of chopped dates or mincemeat. If you use mincemeat, decrease the water a bit. (I don't know what "a bit" is—you are on your own.)

Use what you want of the dough, put the rest in the freezer for another day. My doctor ate 6 of these cookies, absentmindedly, while he was taking by blood pressure and poking at me the other day, though. So maybe you should bake it all.

GRANDMOTHER EMERY'S WINE DROPS

Another Male is Dr. Walter Spofford, a raptor expert, an ornithologist of note, as well as a medical man. His wife, "Dr. Sally," was right-hand woman and Girl Friday for Dr. Arthur Allen, who started and made famous the Cornell Laboratory of Ornithology. At the Spoffords' Arizona home, I watch unbelievingly as tanagers, road runners, hummingbirds, foxes, skunks, javelinas, one year a bobcat come to their door for handouts. Birds of dozens of species flit through their cottonwoods, elf owls call at night, the spectacular Elegant trogon arrived each year from Mexico to nest a few miles down the road until an overabundance of birdwatchers coming to admire and photograph them drove them away. I can sit all day watching the incredible species of hummingbird that blur about their feeders, enjoying their calories while I nibble on mine. Spoff is a fair cook when he has to be, but "these are from his Grandmother Emery's recipe," says Sally, setting a second plate in front of us. "It makes a lot. Spoff carries a tin of them in the van when he goes hawking, in case he forgets to come home for lunch—or because they are his favorite. He says the sherry and nuts sustain him."

Cream 1½ cups of sugar with 1 pound of butter. Add 3 beaten eggs, 1 pound each of raisins, chopped dates, and wal-nuts, 1 teaspoon of baking soda in 2 tablespoons of hot water, ½ cup of sherry, 3 cups of flour, a dash of salt, and "spices to taste," instructed Grandmother. Bake 7 to 8 minutes at 350°.

TOM HALBERG'S BOOKSHOP BARS

To finish up on Cookies, go back to Sweets.

One autumn, seven of us were living and cooking in a small cottage at Edith Andrews's Mothball Pines Banding Station on Nantucket. I told you about that when I was discussing Eggs Benedict. A quiet bookshop manager from the Midwest felt he should contribute to the meals we women were turning out. On a rainy day he stirred up the following and—by demand—almost every day after that. If he left them on a kitchen counter, no matter how small he cut them, how val-iantly we tried to limit ourselves to just one, they would be gone by suppertime and he had to make a second batch. He turned out to be a good cook with other sustenance, but it is those Bars we remember him best for.

Cream 1 cup of shortening with ½ cup each of brown and

white sugar. Add 2 egg yolks, 1 cup of flour, 1 cup of rolled oats. Put this in a greased and floured 9″ × 9″ pan, and bake it at 350° for 20 to 25 minutes. Cut this into bars. Melt 6 ounces of semisweet chocolate with 2 tablespoons of butter. Spread this over the cooled bars, sprinkle the top with chopped nuts or wheat germ. And hide until suppertime.

RITA'S ICED PUMPKIN BARS

Rita has a ballet dancer's figure, a fine sense of color, a husband and three children, runs a hairdressing shop. And any holiday or celebration finds appropriate goodies, flowers, and punch on her counter. "Certainly I like to cook," she says, snipping by my ears. "Would you like the Pumpkin Bars you are eating in your book? We are cross-country skiers, not bird-watchers, but we often see birds in the woods and stop to look at them. The recipe makes a *lot*—you might cut it in half.

"Beat four eggs with two-thirds cup of sugar, one cup of oil, one sixteen-ounce can of pumpkin until fluffy. Then beat in two cups of flour mixed with two teaspoons each of baking powder and cinnamon, one teaspoon each of salt and baking soda. Bake this in a large pan [15″ × 10″] at three hundred fifty degrees for thirty minutes. Cool and frost."

I had just come from the dentist and protested feebly.

"But of course you frost it—that's part of it," she said sternly. "A cake without frosting is like a kiss without a squeeze."

So that's what you should remember about all these sweet foods—the squeeze that makes for happiness.

Cakes

Cookies are easier to make, to serve, to carry with you than cakes (I didn't think of those Pumpkin Bars as cake, though I guess maybe they are). But you can't have a cookbook without one or two real cakes in it. So I'll offer a few—from a simple pound cake to the other end of the scale. (There are two more back where I talked about gingerbread—Buttermilk Cake, which is middle of the Weight Load, and Carrot Cake.)

ANNE PALK'S ROADSIDE CAKE

I was happily autographing my books for customers in a small California bookship. At the end of the afternoon the proprietess slid a plate of lemon cake I'd been ignoring toward me.

"It's special," she said, moving the bowl of camellias between us. "Try it."

I'd given a book program in the morning, been fed a sumptuous Chinese luncheon in a roomful of people I didn't know, then late, hurrying, had become confused and lost in the rabbit warren of stairs, flowers, alleys, art galleries, boutiques of what used to be the small, simple village of Carmel. The last thing my digestion need was cake. But—

"Delicious," I said sincerely. "Why is it special?"

Anne twinkled. "I wasn't going to tell you, We were afraid you'd be formal—lady authors come in all varieties, you might not be amused. This morning while I packed the flowers and teacups and a briefcase in my car, I set the cake on the car roof, forgot it, and drove off. A friend rushed back an hour later and found it lying by the roadside—one half flattened and imprinted by a tire, the other half, once we'd peeled the plastic off and trimmed it, undamaged."

We laughed. Everyone within hearing took a slice. I saw to it mine was the largest.

Serve with humor and apologies. Until the final operation, this was a regular pound cake.

Grease well a springform pan (the kind with a hole in the middle), and heat the oven to 350°. Beat 2 stickes of softened butter with 2 cups of sugar until light; add 2 cups of flour, then 5 eggs, one at a time, beating well after each addition. Pour the batter into the pan, then knock the pan on the counter to settle the mixture. Bake 50 to 60 minutes or until a tester comes out clean. Wait 10 minutes before unmolding. When it is cool, wrap it tightly and store it overnight, but NOT on your car roof.

ROSE AINSWORTH'S MOCHA CAKE

For some years, I summered in the Adirondacks, in deep woods in a lake country thick with birds. Loon flew over at dawn, calling. Canada geese panhandled at the boat docks, a bittern pumped in the marsh. Vireos and warblers and waxwings were everywhere. Morning and evening, I would walk up a woods road to Rose Ainsworth's farmhouse. Her husband had set tree-swallow boxes on poles about his garden to cut down on the mosquitoes and black flies that plagued him. Whitethroat nested in the tangles of his shrubbery. I was studying these birds. The best place to watch them was from Rose's kitchen window, even if fragrances coming from her oven distracted me. Her Mocha Cake was famous, surprisingly easy to make, though mine never turned out like hers. Perhaps her wood stove made the difference. Or was it the walk through the quiet woods, jays scolding in the trees above me, the deer that raised their heads as I passed, slipped between trees, that made her cake taste so good when she slid it, crisp and hot from her stove? We would call her husband in from his wood-pile, not waiting for lunch hour. Rose Ainsworth's Mocha Cake. No icing needed.

Rose melted 3 squares of chocolate in 1⅛ cups of strong hot coffee added to ¾ cup of shortening creamed with 2¾ cups of sugar; ¾ cup of sour cream, ¾ teaspoon of baking soda mixed with 3 cups of cake flour, 1½ teaspoons of vanilla, ¾ teaspoon of salt. She mixed all this, then folded in 5 egg whites, and baked the cake at 350° for 35 to 60 minutes, depending upon her pan and probably upon the heat of her stove.

MARTHA MILLER'S HOLIDAY ALL-FRUIT CAKE

Every year at Christmas, Martha made for her small daughter a Gingerbread House complete with ribbon-candy fencing, lollipop trees, fruit-drop flowers, window boxes, wreaths, lights inside. A lot of trouble. For her friends—also a lot of trouble—she made fruitcake that had barely enough flour to dust the pans. We loved her.

In a huge bowl, she gathered 2 pounds of whole pitted dates, ½ pound each of green and red candied cherries, 1 pound of candied pineapple, and 2 pounds of nuts "soaked in a good-sized wine glass of brandy" (to cover 2 pounds of nuts, it would have to be "good-sized"!). When she considered the nuts soaked, she threw them and the brandy over the fruit and let the bowl sit, covered, overnight. Next day, she added 1½ cups each of flour and sugar, 1 teaspoon of baking powder, and ½ teaspoon of salt, and stirred in 5 large eggs, kneading the mixture with her hands. Her small tins were well greased, lined with paper, greased again. She pressed the mixture firmly in the pans to avoid air pockets, set them in a large pan filled with 1½" of water, and placed them in a preheated 300° oven. The pans were covered for the first hour, then uncovered for another hour.

I don't know who has time or a mixing bowl or wine glass big enough to make this any more, but we were all mighty sad when her daughter outgrew Gingerbread Houses and Martha moved to another part of the country.

ATCHIE ALEXANDER'S FRUIT-NUT TORTE

From Cataloochee Ranch in the Great Smokies. Splendidly unhealthy, but if you have been on a horse all day, that won't matter.

Our last child was safe at college; my husband was leaving for a two-week fishing trip. Wholly free for the first time of my household duties, I went adventurously on a two-week riding trip in the Great Smokies. I square-danced with champions, avoided rattlesnakes, controlled a runaway steed, and had a glorious time with interesting people who didn't know or care that I was a wife and mother. I returned to find the daughter bedded in the college infirmary from an emergency appendectomy; her father's fishing trip had been canceled—he was living in a cold and empty house. The trophies I brought home (besides dreams of my square-dancing partner) were a leaking bottle of moonshine wrapped in dirty shirts and socks, and the recipe for Atchie's cake. I hope she won't mind my passing it on. It can be kept a month or eaten the day after baking.

Mix 3 eggs, 1 cup of vegetable oil, 1½ cups of sugar, 2 cups of flour, 1 teaspoon each of baking soda, salt, nutmeg, allspice, and cinnamon. Add 1 cup of buttermilk, 1 cup of cooked prunes, 2 teaspoons of vanilla, 2 teaspoons of baking powder, 1 cup of walnut meats (preferably black, which are more available in Tennessee). Bake in a shallow greased pan at 300°. It will take 55 minutes at a high altitude, less at sea level. When it comes out of the oven, spike holes in it and pour over the following hot sauce that has been boiled to the soft-ball stage: 1 cup of sugar, ½ cup of buttermilk, ¼ cup of oil, 1 teaspoon of vanilla, and ½ teaspoon of baking soda. You can serve this plain or, if you aren't counting calories, with whipped cream. (But by now you've stopped counting the calories in this, so why not slather it with whipped cream? You can ride, if you are in the Smokies, or hike it off the next day. Going birding wouldn't be brisk enough. There are thrashers singing from every bush on those hills.)

BRIDGET GALLAGHER'S CAKE

And, finally, partly because it feeds so many, is so much in demand for "Bird Suppers," but mostly because its story stirs my emotions, re-creates for me the loneliness and courage of a woman who every afternoon scattered grain for hundreds of waterfowl that flew on beating wings down a Colorado lake to her feet, I want to give you Bridget Gallagher's Cake. She was old. I hope she died before burgeoning development, city people urbanizing, clearing her tranquil lake shores, brought knowledge of water pollution and laws against feeding ducks and geese. For years, she and her husband had studied the birds that nested on their rural marshy islands and shoreline, had counted the migrating birds—great skeins of geese, ducks; shore birds feeding by the reeds; songbirds, warblers flying from one continent to another. She knew them all. Now that she was alone, a small woman walking with a cane, for company she fed birds lavishly, hoped the Audubon Society could continue this when she was gone, use her home for a nature center. Although development crowded daily closer, she and a few neighboring ranchers had kept their land wild.

Two Staff and I went there on an inspection trip one hot afternoon. Bridget led us about her boundaries, told us of the birds ordinary and rare she and her husband had listed over the years, pointed out the native flora and plantings they had made for wildlife. She showed us meadows they kept clear for field species, a guesthouse that might serve for offices. At the end, as we sat on her porch drinking welcomed iced tea; she offered us double helpings of a chocolate cake—moist, delicious. I pressed her for its recipe. I'm not much on cakes, but I really wanted this. She laughed shyly and took my address. "I'll have to look it up," she said, "but I promise."

It wasn't until she reached for her iced-tea glass, which one of the men had moved, that we realized she could not see it—she was blind.

Two weeks later, her recipe reached me at home inside a weighty Priority Mail package that contained, in its 8″ × 10″ pan, her cake. I've made it often since, thinking of this woman, her lake, her land, her anxiety about her birds, the bulldozers.

Mix 2 cups of flour, 2 cups of sugar, 2 teaspoons of cinnamon, 1 teaspoons of baking soda. Pour over this 1 cup of water, 2 sticks of margarine, and 2 tablespoons of cocoa, all of which have been brought to a boil. Add 2 eggs and ½ cup of buttermilk, beat the batter well, and spread it in a large pan. While it is baking for about 25 minutes in a 350° oven, mix 1 stick of shortening, 4 tablespoons of cocoa, ½ cup of buttermilk, 1 box of sugar, 1 teaspoon of vanilla. Spoon this over the cake when you take it from the oven. It will cover it thickly, then sink in. Decorate the top with walnuts or almonds, coconut or colored jimmies, as desired. This keeps well—at least until birdwatchers arrive.

TORTA DE ZAPALLO

Oh, all right—I'll be generous and give you one more cake—a Conversation Dish.

To 1½ pounds of peeled and cubed pumpkin or winter squash (or two packages of frozen squash), add 1 cup of sugar, ½ cup of heavy cream, ½ teaspoon of cinnamon, 1 cup of raisins, 1 cup of grated muenster, 3 large eggs, 2 ounces of dark rum. Grease your pan liberally, and bake for about 1 hour at 350°. Pour another ounce of rum over this, and serve with whipped cream, sour cream, or ice cream. (I told you it is a Conversation Cake.)

Drinks

Healthy Drinks

Someone will always want coffee, which means you must remember to buy cream, which you will then be stuck with (you can put it in a casserole later). But people have been drinking coffee all day. You need that big coffee pot for other liquids. Don't spoil him/her—provide Instant Coffee. In the excitement or out of good manners, he/she won't notice. (A write would have an easier time if there were only one sex, but who wants that?)

For those who are apprehensive of mulled cider or a pitcher that might contain spirits (you needn't tell them about the wine in the stew you will shortly serve), tea is equally simple to make. Tea, these days, comes in bags of an infinite variety. It is no longer (or at least not usually) made, the way Mother taught you—rinsing cups and teapot with boiling water, polishing the silver—but it's satisfactory.

SUN TEA

The least effort—I'm thinking of hot weather, of iced tea—
is Sun Tea. This is thriftily made by setting a glass jar in the
sun with the requisite amount of tea for the amount of water.
Mint or herbs can be added to this, and frozen lemonade, which
will sweeten it.

SASSAFRAS TEA

In colonial times, magnificent stands, up to sixty feet tall,
of *Sassafras variifolium* grew on Cape Cod. The Indians knew
it well, had a score of medicinal uses for it, steeping the bark
for teas, crushing leaves for poultices to stop bleeding. When
word of this miracle tree and its uses reached England, it became
touted as a cure-all and a fashionable luxury brew. The colonists chopped their beneficial source of riches with eager axes
and exported it to such an extent that today it is a botanical
rarity found only in a few places as a small, shrublike sapling.
Its three-formed mitten leaves are a source of interest to children. The new, soft ones are good to chew. Supposedly healthy,
my mother taught me, picking spring tips along the edges of
the Chestnut Hill Golf Course near Boston. The chestnuts,
the golf course, and the sassafras are gone, but when you can
find it, you can (if you wish) make a tonic from the rosy outer
bark of the roots steeped in boiling water. When this colors,
becomes dark, strain it, add sugar, and serve it to your birding
and botanical friends as a curiosity, which it certainly now is.
Six cups of boiling water to 4 large pieces of bark and 6 teaspoons of sugar.

Since my woodland yields no sassafrass I have been known—but not twice—to serve Ginger Tea to birders with a cold. Birders are always rushing outside inadequately clothed, eat irregularly, cram into cars with others unwilling to stay home because they have the sniffles. Ginger Tea gives them something to talk about other than their nasal miseries. Add ½ teaspoon each of ground ginger, honey, and lemon juice to 1 cup of boiling water and 1 or 2 grains of salt. I don't say you have to like this—it's supposedly medicinal.

Easier, perhaps, on the throat is an infusion of Parsley Tea, which my herb-medicine friends claim will cure anything. They say thyme is good for hangovers, too, quoting Carolus Linnaeus, but they haven't given me a liquid recipe. This is perhaps because they know my personal remedy for respiratory problems is rum lemonades with honey. The honey, my father-in-law taught me, soothes the throat, the lemon cuts phlegm, the rum gives a glow to the hours and induces naps. If you have to lie around snuffling, why not be comfortable?

MULLED CIDER

Socially more welcomed, equally simple, also healthy, for cold days.

I still remember a huge kettle of mulled cider, the steam and fragrance that rose from it, in Taffy's California hall one noon, when a group of us straggled in, arguing about some murres we had seen. The kettle was big enough to absorb our weariness, wipe out the scrounginess of our failures and car trouble. Some days, some places, some murres you remember better than others. Maybe her cider wasn't better than others I have had, but I've made the simple recipe ever since.

All you do is add cinnamon sticks and whole cloves and 1 slice of lemon to 1 gallon of cider. Maybe 3 sticks, 12 cloves. Warm this, then set it over low heat or on an electric plate.

SPICED COFFEE

Similar, but different.

Add 6 sticks of cinnamon, 12 cloves, and a few strips of orange peel to an 8-cup drip basket with your usual coffee in it. Plop a spoonful of whipped cream into each mug when serving. If you want to add this recipe to the next category, there *are* birders who like a spoonful of brandy or rum with their orange peel.

EGGNOG HOT AND SPICED

Richer. No liquor.

To 2 cups of eggnog, add 1 cup of milk, 1 cinnamon stick, and 2 whole cloves. Heat to simmering only, remove the spices, and keep the drink warm. See the comment above on an "extra spoonful" to ensure warmth.

WARM PUNCH

For cold people at 11:00 A.M., when it is perhaps too early for wine. Healthy, but can be adjusted.

Mull equal amounts of cranberry and orange juice with thin lemon slices, 1 tablespoon of sugar, a shake each of cinnamon and nutmeg. You should stand a bottle of white wine beside this in case you have misjudged your visitors.

SPICED WINE

For cold people at 4:00 P.M.

To 2 bottles dry red wine, add 3 cored, peeled, and thinly sliced apples, 3 whole cloves, 2 cinnamon sticks, ½ cup of sugar, 1 teaspoon of lemon juice. This also can be kept warm and smells hospitably marvelous. Serves 10.

IRISH COFFEE

Sweet and sustaining at any hour.

A mug of hot coffee, sugar, a shot of bourbon, whipped cream. This can be changed by using a drop or two—not too much—of Kahlúa, Amaretto, or spiced rum (more of the rum).

FRUIT PUNCH

This is made from orange, pineapple and/or cranberry, apricot, any of the suitable tropical fruits such as papaya and mango, Surinam cherry, but always with lemon and lime added. The usual proportion is 4 to 5 cups of juice to 1 quart of ginger ale or wine. Figure on 2 cups to a person (3 is certainly safer), with an extra supply at hand. Float lemon, orange, strawberries, pineapple, white grapes in this for decoration. Instead of using ice cubes, freeze bowls of water with a handful of fruit in each. This is decorative, doesn't water the punch as much as cubes will. But be aware that you can't wait until the last minute to prepare them. With any mixed group, it is mannerly to have two bowls—one with, one without alcohol.

POTOPAUG PUNCH FOR BIRD, BUTTERFLY, AND BRIDAL-PARTY WATCHERS

Combine 6 cups of pineapple, 2 cups of cranberry, 1 cup of lemon juice; add 1 cup of sugar. Stir in at the last minute 2 quarts of ginger ale or white wine. Have an ample stock of gallon jugs, filled, waiting in the wings.

CRANBERRY PUNCH

To 1 quart of cranberry or pineapple juice, add 1 8-ounce can each of frozen lemon and orange juice. Just before serving, pour in 1 quart of club soda with as much vodka added as seems suitable for your group.

ROSEMARY PUNCH FOR WEDDINGS

Has benefits other than cooling the throat, protecting against the evil eye, declaring fidelity, refreshing memory. Before modern medicine, rosemary was used as a stimulant, a carminative (not useful at weddings), to relieve headaches, bruises, and nervous tension—all of which can accompany weddings. It grows, the ancient belief is, only in the gardens of the righteous. Mourners should throw it into your grave.

If there is any punch left over, it is said to make a good moth repellent.

Boil for 5 minutes 1 quart of water, 4 cups of sugar, 3 tablespoons of dried rosemary leaves, ¼ cup of lemon juice. Strain the mixture, and cool it. Then add 2 cups of lime juice, 2 cups of lemon juice, and 2 quarts of strawberries that have been sliced thinly or put through a sieve. Here, the father of the bride must decide whether to add 2 quarts of white wine or of water with the necessary 20 ounces of ginger ale and the ice. It's a matter of his nervous tension.

Revivifying Drinks

PORGE'S PUNCH

My friend Porge, craftswoman and magnificent cook, once ran a boardinghouse with her artist-husband on a bleak headland on a far peninsula of the Maine coast. Since they catered to birdwatchers, they were sensitive to their needs and desires at that hour of dusk when guests gather in front of a fire, tantalized by the fragrances of the dinner to come, refreshing themselves from pitchers on the coffee tables.

To 1 pint of brandy (apricot, preferably) Porge added 1 bottle each of Sauternes and dry champagne, and, for the "Ladies Pitcher," 1 quart of soda water. Her comment was that women preferred the first three ingredients mixed with soda water (or ginger ale), men preferred them mixed with nothing.

SANGRÍA

"You haven't told them," says my friend Rudolph, proofreading this section for me, "about adding a shot of Midori to a glass of orange juice. Any woman should like that—Midori is the color of melon, a lovely green."

"Before you mix it," countered Terry, who was proofreading "Soups." "It changes color. And how about that liqueur I put out last night—a little Sambuca, not much, slipped into Irish Cream?" These men are fishermen, not birders. But since they also must be up and out early, go casting for bass well past midnight, hot soup and liquors and birders' fare are applicable to them. They are tolerant of us.

"I suppose," they asked, "beer is too ordinary for you to put in your book? On a hot day, when you are out at sea scouting for pelagic birds, don't you take a cooler of it with you? You haven't put in Sangría either. That's refreshing at the end of a hot afternoon, and not too strong. What kind of a Birdwatcher's Cookbook is this?"

"It's going to be a six-hundred-page one if people don't stop pressing recipes on me," I moaned. "I can't use everything I know. But you're right about Sangría—a lot of people like it.

Combine ⅔ cup of lemon juice or frozen lemonade with 1 cup of orange juice, ¼ cups of sugar syrup—less if you use frozen lemonade (it's sweetened). Mix this in a pitcher—glass, for visual attraction—with ½ gallon of Gallo burgundy, ⅓ cup of Cointreau, ¼ cup of brandy, and serve it with a splash of sparkling water. This keeps, chilled.

FATHER FISK'S RUM PUNCH

At the other end of the scale from Sun Tea and Mulled Cider is this Rum Punch. I can't close this section without giving you my personal recipe, although, as I've said, I use what is at hand and don't measure. This potion has seen me through weddings and funerals, celebrations and crises. May it do the same for others. I'd rather my mourners used it than rosemary. I don't want them wasting any by pouring it into my grave.

To 2 cups each of orange, cranberry, and pineapple juice add 2 cups of strong tea (you can steep cloves in this, but it isn't necessary), ½ cup of frozen lemonade, and 2 fifths of dark rum. And, of course, ice. In the Caribbean, we used lime juice and added the clear fluid from a pipa—a green, or barely ripe, coconut. If the measuring wasn't accurate, the results were predictable—guaranteed to make me dream in delight of pelicans, ant shrikes, and elaenias.

If you are driving, perhaps you should stick to Mulled Cider. This goes for Terry's Sambuca slipped into Irish Cream, too.

CHRISTMAS-COUNT PICKUP

By dark on Christmas-Count Night, the teams assemble to report on their tallies. They have been drinking coffee all day, they are in the mood for something more revivifying.

Clear and relatively healthy.

Combine 1 gallon of cider, 1 quart of cranberry juice, 2 cups of orange juice, 1 cup of lemon juice (use frozen lemonade, and decrease the sugar), 1 cup (or less) of sugar, 2 teaspoons each of cloves and allspice, 3 cinnamon sticks. Put these in an outsized coffeepot with the sugar and spices in the basket, and perk as you would coffee. Add a jigger of rum or brandy to each mug when serving (this is important).

CHRISTMAS EGGNOG

And, of course, there is the traditional Christmas Eggnog, not necessarily Healthy. Christmas comes but once a year, and it will soothe your weariness, make that bird species you hunted all day but never found seem less important. Sweet, nourishing, it is also deceptive. So if you are going to be driving home, keep count.

Making an Eggnog is a celebratory occasion. There ought to be an Eggnog Moon as there is a Harvest Moon. Before your jugs are filled, the kitchen is awash with eggshells, measuring cups, miscounted evaporated milk tins, bottles, spilled sugar, and supervisory helpers. Each year I look up the proper proportions, try to figure them for the unknown number of people I may be serving. There are recipes in cookbooks, December magazine advertisements, those giveaway booklets you find at liquor stores, the tips of friendly tongues—male. Then you double or triple. If you have any left over, New Year's is coming; you need to give a second party anyway. My trouble is that halfway through my mixing, the telephone rings or a neighbor stops by and distracts me. I lose count. Some years I use real cream—the kind that won't make butter if it sits overnight, as Grandmother's did, but that has body to it; some years I don't. I use equal amounts of dark rum, bourbon, and brandy. I make up gallons a day or two ahead so the contents mellow, trying not to let them mellow me, too. Neighbors down my lane give a traditional Christmas party each year, complete with bells, long dresses, trees, mixed ages, lots of chocolates, babies crawling on the floor, carol singing, teenagers whooping in and out, food and drink for all ages, and *lots* of eggnog. Fortunately, I live near enough to walk home.

The proportions they use are (Harold wrinkled his brow when he was telling me—he says he loses count sometimes, too) 1 dozen eggs, separated—the beaten whites added at the end—1 cup (he thinks) of sugar, 10 cups of evaporated milk diluted with 3 or 4 cups of water (Harold wrinkled his brow again). Or, if you prefer, 2 quarts of cream. Then 1½ cups each of brandy, bourbon, and rum. The amount of this last depends upon the kinds of guests he is serving—he reduces or increases it. "Sailors, fishermen, and, I expect, birdwatchers get more"; his wife's relatives and young people less. "Put it in a cool place to ripen; shake nutmeg on each cup when you serve it." He patted my shoulder as I wrote this down. "You can't go wrong."

SUSAN'S CHRISTMAS GLÖGG

In really cold country, instead of eggnog you can keep a kettle of Christmas Glögg on your stove and ladle that out.

The raisins and almonds at the bottom are deceptive—it is a really intoxicating drink. Susan serves it in her home on a bluff overlooking the ocean. Outside, far below, waves crash against snowy rocks. Inside, her rooms festive with firelight, candles, green boughs, and people. She asks each guest to bring a plate of tidbits, which has become competitive—we eat very well, even if in small bites. It isn't until I get outside later, hunting for my car, that I realize Glögg is a product of Sweden, where the people are hardy and need insulation against Weather. I stand on the edge of the bluff, letting the winter wind clear my head, look back at Susan's windows, warm with their Christmas cheer, wave to a man who has come to the doorway. What had been in that drink besides raisins and almonds?

"It's my father's recipe," she told me another day. "He's Norwegian; it has come down in the family. The Swedes claim they invented Glögg—it's an argument. The proportions are four parts port to one part bourbon. You start by simmering spices in a cheesecloth bag in maybe a cup of water for ten to fifteen minutes—three pieces of orange peel, twelve whole cloves, one cinnamon stick, one whole nutmeg, one table-spoon of cardamom seeds. Those are tiny—they come in pods. It's the children's job to extract them—that's traditional, too. While the spices are simmering, set one-half gallon of port to heat. Add as many raisins (two cups) as you want and one tablespoon of sugar. When the port is almost boiling, add the spice liquid, a cup or more of almonds, and one pint of bour-bon. Continue heating this, and, when it is really hot, ignite it to burn off the alcohol—just for a minute or two—then clap on the kettle cover, and keep it warm. For a party like mine, I triple this. Everyone brings food, I have coffee, too, and the road in here is so winding that by the time people reach the highway, they are in good shape. *You* walked off in the wrong direction. I worried for a moment, then realized you had gone to look at the ocean, those terrific breakers that night, crashing in the moonlight. Ted checked on you, until you came back to your car." I thanked her. Not many people worry about me.

COUPE?

And, finally, it's just as well I don't know what this is called, it's better I don't go asking for it. Some kind of a coupe.

In New York one day, a pleasant young man shepherded me under his umbrella to a restaurant near the National Audubon Society, where we had been working. We each ordered a normal light lunch, and, because I still had much to accomplish, I requested my usual luncheon milk. The waiter looked a bit astonished but returned with a gobletful, setting down with more of a flourish in front of my companion a goblet not entirely similar. Fragrance wafted across the table; my eyebrow raised. Fred laughed and pushed the drink toward me.

"It's a celebration, having lunch together. I'd like to order you one. Try it." Sipping, I decided getting about New York had enough dangers without adding this to them. But I kept eyeing it—that sip had been delicious. When it was time for dessert, which I don't eat—

"I want one of those," I recanted. "And I want it at the bar. I *have* to see what goes into it. I don't believe what you have told me."

The young bartender, pleased by my interest, amused by my skepticism, showed off his skill. He arched first a stream of Kahlúa into a blender, then white Crème de Cacao, then half-and-half, then—this was harder—Hershey's Syrup, which is heavy (his arc had to be shortened). Grinning at my expres-

sion, unbelievably he added a large spoonful of *peanut butter*—
I could swear it was Skippy! He blended all of this with crushed
ice and started to pour it out.

"Two goblets," I ordered firmly. "Half of *that* will be plenty
of dessert for me." As he set them in front of us, I questioned
my companion anxiously. "Will you be able to get me back to
the office in the rain? It's not me I'm worrying about. It's
you—if you drink that."

To the last drop I sucked through the straw, pulling on it
at the end like a child. "Coupe Something." I'm not about to
serve it at a Birdwatchers party. I'm waiting to celebrate something important—like having a manuscript accepted, winning
a lottery, or sitting on a couch in front of a fire with a carefully
chosen, affectionate companion.

FRAPPÉ FOR FIFTY

From a crumbling paper booklet of 1908, *Choice Receipts,
Thoroughly Tested and Reliable, of the Ladies of Ortonville, Minnesota* (where, on page 1, readers are instructed to boil String
Beans—2 hours; Beets, 3½ hours; Parsnips, Squash, and Turnips, 1 hour; Potatoes and Green Peas, ½ hour; also to "add a

sufficient quantity of flour"—and often brandy—to their cookies), comes the following Frappé. It is very similar, if a suitable amount of wine is substituted, to the above Party Punches.

Blend (in 1908, a fruit press did this) 8 bananas, 8 oranges, and the juice of 12 lemons with 1½ boxes of strawberries (size of box not specified), reserving ½ box. Add 4 cups of sugar and 2 quarts of water; stir until the sugar has dissolved. Cut up and add 4 more oranges, 4 more bananas with the reserved strawberries and some cracked ice.

To give myself courage to face those bananas (one Ortonville lady, I was pleased to discover, used grated pineapple), I *could* make myself and any guest a lunch of Kalops—a stew, I judge, of "any small scraps of beef floured, seasoned, scattered with cut onions and bay leaves, with water poured down one side," cooked slowly. "Very savory," commented the ladies.

I'd be more apt, though, to stir up—as good now as in 1908—an entrée of 1 cup of canned corn, chopped fine, 2 egg yolks, onion, and ½ green pepper, sautéed with seasonings, folded into 1 cup of steamed rice, then layered in a casserole with ½ cup of grated cheese, baked for 12 minutes at 500°. The Minnesota Ladies probably didn't use the garlic and hot salsa I'd consider essential, but some of my luncheon ladies wouldn't either, although they would appreciate my substitution of wild rice.

I found equally modern receipts used by those good Ladies, but my attention was constantly distracted by instructions for Cough Syrup, Communion Wine, Chapped Hands, Frost Bite

Cure, culminating in a full, handwritten page on the making of Rose Beads, which are started with rose petals ground in a meat cutter three times daily for nine days. Supportive advertisements in the booklet urged the ladies to remember "A RAINY DAY IS COMING" (this from a bank), claims that the "BIG STONE COUNTY JOURNAL" was one "you can safely admit into your family circle," promises that "THE TEMPERANCE HOTEL is A GOOD DOLLAR A DAY HOUSE with plenty of reading matter."

Tidbits and Snacks

The best cocktail accompaniments (to my mind) are platters of really good cheeses, sharp knives, and crackers that don't break: And vegetables set about a bowl of one of the dozens of dips that friends, cookbooks, and market shelves offer. But since housewives (and househusbands) are always looking for ways to avoid answering the piles of letters on their desks, I'll suggest the following.

Cold

DIPS, SPREADS, ETC.

Keep a supply of cream cheese on hand. It can be softened with sour cream, yogurt, or mayonnaise—in an emergency, even with milk. Add chutney, blue cheese, and Worcestershire sauce to give texture and taste. The only recipe I refused to divulge in our government days was my cocktail dip. It was so easy, so quick, I didn't want to find myself meeting it in every home I went to. All I did was soften cream cheese with chili sauce and smile secretively when seafood or other exotic ingredients were guessed. When I had time, I added finely chopped celery and grated onion, but often there was no time. Almost anything can be successfully used with cream cheese or sour cream—even a little horseradish. There's not room in this book to list the variety.

Vegetable platters are colorful, but you are limited to what you can pick up neatly in your fingers. You can win Brownie points by adding sliced jícama—round, brown, smooth tubers that come from Mexico; or Jerusalem artichokes—knobby brown tubers that grow below those tall, sunflowerlike plants in the far corner of my garden (if I *can* keep these in the far corner—they multiply like mice). Both of these are crisp, white, the texture maybe of water chestnuts—with more flavor.

Both dips and vegetables leave you free to be in the living room, laughing with your guests instead of hovering in the kitchen trying to broil without burning whatever—usually a cheese or the equivalent of a dip—you have put on squares of bread.

Cream cheese also is a base for cheese balls, which can be

made up days ahead of time and kept until needed. These are different kinds of cheese, blended, seasoned with curry, brandy, sherry—whatever your whim of the day is—firmed into balls of appropriate size, then rolled in crushed walnuts, or olives and parsley, or sesame seeds. They are attractive on a bed of greens, and it is fun to slice into one, try to decide what your hostess uses that you may not. Any left over can be refirmed, rounded, rolled again.

I have an editor who peels a ripe avocado neatly, coats it with a little mayonnaise, and scatters sesame seeds on it. This keeps us in the kitchen admiring him and must take him all of 5 minutes—from peeling to cutting in bite-sized pieces.

I used to make my own liver pâté, cooking chicken livers, blending them with onion and hardboiled egg, brandy, and curry. This would go into a bowl plain or be encased in jellied consommé with parsley and decorative slices of stuffed olives. Then I discovered that a good liverwurst mixed with a little sour cream, a little grated onion, 2 tablespoons of fresh parsley, and 2 tablespoons of bourbon was accepted without demur and was far less trouble. Just don't forget the bourbon.

STUFFED EGGS

These were supposed to ring the vegetable platters. I forgot. Instead of just mashing mustard and mayonnaise with the yolks, add finely chopped parsley and chives, or mushrooms and curry, or chili sauce, or anchovy paste (a little). I hope you are more deft at stuffing eggs than I am.

MIDDLE EAST GARBANZO SPREAD

Probably international in lands where chickpeas grow.

Cook 1 cup of garbanzos (chickpeas) until they are tender, or buy canned ones. Purée in some of their liquid 1 onion and 2 minced garlic cloves that have been lightly sautéed. (Now you are back to cooking.) Add salt, lemon juice, and ½ cup of roasted sesame seeds.

MOLLY'S SPINACH DIP

Excellent for lunch, good with salads and soups, a sturdy base at cocktail parties. Any of her friends who have been to parties in her small apartment, where they sit on the floor and secondhand furniture never meant to accommodate such gatherings, will recognize it. She isn't a birder but contributed this one weekend to one of my parties. I've used it ever since.

Thaw, drain, and chop 1 package of frozen spinach or its fresh equivalent. Add 1 cup each of sour cream and mayonnaise, 1 package of Knorr Vegetable Soup Mix, and let this sit overnight or all day. Neatly hollow out a loaf of French or rye bread, fill it with the dip, and use the pieces you have cut from the bread for dipping. You can change this dish into a full meal by adding red and green peppers, chopped onion, and 1 cup or more of finely chopped ham, chicken, or bacon. By then, I suppose, it is a grinder, topless.

Hot

Those cold accompaniments to drinks let me mingle and chat with my friends. There are a few easy hot ones.

CORNELL LABORATORY OF ORNITHOLOGY CHEESE LOGS

May not be entirely hot by the time you manage to get one, but they will be warm and so good that you won't mind. They are sort of a cheese ball to begin with—just treated differently.

Cream ¼ cup of butter with 1 cup of grated Cheddar, 1 cup of flour, salt, red pepper (important), ¼ teaspoon of curry or onion, ¾ cup of chopped walnuts. Shape this into logs, chill them thoroughly, slice them thinly, and bake at 325° for about 10 minutes. Like cheese balls, these keep well and can be frozen. Reheat them slightly before serving, if you can't pass them around straight out of the oven.

HOT CRAB MEAT

The best. Should be served really hot, but it's worth staying in the kitchen. People will be there with you anyway, pouring drinks or hoping to find a quiet spot to chat.

Mix 1 pound of crab meat with 8 ounces of cream cheese, 1 tablespoon of minced onion, 1 teaspoon of horseradish, curry, and a dash of Worcestershire sauce. Adjust the amounts for the size of your group, but your guests will snatch more than you may plan on. This can be served as a dip with crackers or on toast squares.

I expect (see page 145) that I tossed sour cream into this. Carelessly.

COCKTAIL MEATBALLS

Combine ½ pound of ground beef with 1 egg, ½ cup of bread stuffing, 1 minced onion, 1 minced garlic clove, black pepper, salt, a dash each of cayenne and nutmeg, horseradish (if you wish). Roll the mixture into small balls, and sauté in 3 tablespoons of hot oil until they are golden brown. Serve, with toothpicks, around a bowl of Parmesan or tomato sauce.

VEGETARIAN COCKTAIL BALLS

They looked like meatballs. Small, brown, crispy. The young man standing by me picked one out of a bean pot with a toothpick, inspected it, put it back.

"It's all right," a Navy wife behind us reassured him. "They are spinach, not beef." The vegetarian, watching carefully as I sampled one, followed suit. Delicious.

All I could obtain in the way of instructions was chopped spinach, cheese, herbed crumbs.

"What kind of cheese?" I pressed.

"Oh—whatever you have."

"What proportions?"

She waved her hands vaguely, disappeared into another room.

Next morning, putting leftovers into soup for lunch, I found some spinach. Less than ½ cup. I drained it, added grated cheese—Cheddar of some sort (it was a leftover, too)—½ cup of crumbs to bind these, a couple of tablespoons of ricotta I'd bought to make a ricotta cake and hadn't yet used, a shake each of garlic salt and oregano, and rolled the mixture into small balls. When a birding couple stopped by that afternoon, I put the balls in a low oven. They weren't crispy like my Navy friend's. What someone else cooks is always better, especially at a cocktail party. I hunted through cookbooks at my bookstore, queried a friend who caters. I hadn't been told about an egg. My next attempt turned out better but lacked the sense of adventure.

To 1 package of frozen spinach, cooked and drained, add 1 cup of herbed stuffing (or your own bread crumbs and herbs), ½ cup of finely chopped onion, 1 finely chopped garlic clove (the garlic is my addition), 2 eggs, ½ cup or more of Parmesan or other cheese. Roll this into small balls; chill. Bake them at 375° for 15 minutes, or drop them into deep fat and fry them until they turn brown. That high heat was how the Navy wife got hers so crispy. I bake them now and keep them crisping in the oven to refill the bean pot I also use to serve them in. It keeps them warm.

Snacks

BRAZIL-NUT CHIPS

"It is advisable," warns Kitty Larmon of New Hampshire, "to pad the inside of the second joint of your index finger on the cutting hand with a Band-Aid. If the telephone rings, and you are interrupted, and the nuts become neglected and dry out, then simmer them again."

Kitty says that when she looks at the news on TV or sits over tea with someone who has come to list the birds at her feeders, she slices Brazil nuts. "Thin, with a *very* sharp knife. They are a nice change from peanuts, and a jar of them makes a gift." She sent me a jarful; they were a gift.

She covers the nuts with cold water, brings them to a boil, simmers them for 20 minutes, drains and pats them dry. With that *very* sharp knife, wearing her Band-Aid, she slices them lengthwise, four or five slices to a nut, dries them again, then stirs them in a glaze made from 1 egg white, 1 teaspoon of water, ¼ teaspoon of salt that has been beaten only until frothy. She spreads the nuts on a greased flat pan—it must be flat, like a cookie sheet, so that the hot air flows over it—and sprinkles them lightly with sea salt. They are baked at 300° for 20 minutes, stirred, and baked, longer until they turn light brown—about 10 minutes. You have to keep checking. "Like anything else in an oven," she says, cheerfully breaking open a roll I had burned for her dinner, "you have to keep a watchful eye."

ALMONDS TERIYAKI

Sounds complicated, but isn't.

Bake in a 325° oven for 5 minutes 2 cups of almonds spread loosely on a baking sheet while you combine 1 tablespoon each of soy sauce and oil, 1 teaspoon each of lemon juice and brown sugar. Stir this until the sugar dissolves, then add ½ teaspoon each of ginger and salt, ¼ teaspoon each of garlic and onion powder. Coat the nuts in the sauce; return them to the oven for 10 minutes, stirring them once. "Keep," as Kitty would say, "a watchful eye." Cool and store them in an airtight tin.

Pelagic Preparations

Except for transportation to the Dry Tortugas from Key West before the days when airplanes started zooming tourists over for a few brief hours (we were serious researchers staying a week and more, going frequently), I have been on only two pelagic trips. One was rough, the weather was bad, we saw nothing. One was balmy, the sun was hot, we saw nothing. I found standing at the rail trying to balance binoculars on an occasional distant speck boring, odors wafting from the fast-food stand nauseating. So I can't advise you on what to take.

"Crackers," says Susan Drennan, editor of *American Birds*. "Lots of crackers."

"Fruit and a cooler with *lots* to drink, nonalcoholic," advises another informant.

"Whatever can be squished into your backpack," comes from another. "Peanut-butter or cream-cheese-and-olive sandwiches aren't too messy."

My favorite male cook raises his eyebrows. "Thinly sliced roast beef with mayonnaise on whole-wheat bread," he drawls. "Why do you need anything more, except beer? Why fuss when that is so good? You women go to too much trouble."

Don't Forget Your Family

Birdwatchers have families; you can at least be as nice to them as you are to your vegetarian friends. If good relationships are to be maintained, if you are to be free to go birding, they need to be provided for. Cater to their tastes and needs. Set aside duplicate chowders, casseroles, stews in dishes ready to be heated up with a minimum of skill. Keep your cookie jar, cheese shelf, and fruit bowls replenished. You love them, don't you? Of course, it *is* good for them occasionally to be independent, to frizzle up their own eggs and hamburger, stew up apples or rhubarb, be proud that they leave a clean kitchen (if they do). If you discover that they have eaten only peanut-butter sandwiches or pizza in your absence, they will be glad to have you return, and what you prepared for them will be ready for *you* to use, saving time and helping to reestablish you as head of the household. Leave them a big bowl of chocolate pudding. The store-bought mix is very quick; if you put a spoonful of Instant Coffee into it, add a dash of rum, they will never know the difference. Suggest they mix it with ice cream to make it go further. Be sure there *is* plenty of ice cream.

Don't Forget the Birds!

While you are off counting birds at someone else's feeders, you have your own back-yard constituents. You attracted them for your pleasure, so you have an obligation to them.

Feeders come in dozens of types, available from five-and-ten-cent stores, markets, garden and hardware departments, nature centers, catalogues. The two only really squirrel-proof ones I have found over many years and efforts are (1) the Droll Yankee large Big Top (be sure it is the large one), which is adjustable so grackles and jays won't sit inside it on fine days as well as rainy, as chickadees and other small birds happily do. Its crystal half dome reflects sky and tree shadows, adding wonderful reflections to your yard. It is relatively easy to clean. (2) My secondhand Hilarious Bird Feeder is harder to clean but defeats even red squirrels, so I forgive this. It, too, is adjustable to keep out larger birds as you wish.

It is important to keep your feeders clean. Diseases spread through bird populations as they do through human. While feeders should be hung near shrubbery so birds needn't fly across big open spaces to reach them, they should be inaccessible to cats. Yes, I know, *your* cat never hunts birds. Someone recently estimated the U.S. cat population at 80 million—80,000,000. (Is that enough zeros?) If each cat catches, however casually, denying its ancestral hunting instinct, only one bird a year, that's 80-million birds, a figure to contemplate in these days of rapidly disappearing habitats.

Water: Let me get this in right away—water is more essential both winter and summer than are feeders. The size of the container—a decorative pool, a shallow dish or hollowed rock, a garbage-pail lid (for some reason, birds love these—I did a study on containers in my yard once—but they must be metal, not slippery plastic)—doesn't matter as long as it slopes to 2, at the most 3, inches deep. The bird is bathing, not swimming. It must be kept clean and placed near protective shrubbery for security. Dripping water is more attractive than still water, whether from a fountain, a waterfall, or just a milk carton with a pinhole in its bottom, hung over a branch.

Food can be as elaborate a project as you wish to make it. You can start—and finish, if you don't want to bother further—with sunflower seeds and cracked corn, the finer the better for the smaller birds. Some species like millet or the black thistle seed, niger, that is imported from India and parts of Africa. There, niger is a staple food crop for people, which is perhaps something we should be aware of when we promote its commercial sale to us for finches. Finches, after all, have kept themselves alive for centuries on a diet of native weed and grass seeds. I grant I enjoy the winter color of goldfinches in my yard, but there are those starving faces that TV likes to show us—usually at mealtime. Finches also like small sunflower seeds, which can be a substitute for niger. They have to work harder, though, and who likes to have to work harder?

Seeds, plain and mixed, are available at feed and bird stores and in many markets. If you buy a mix, some of it may prove to be filler, not relished by the birds of your locality. It's rather fun to put different kinds in small dishes and study who eats what. In Florida, the 1,200 painted buntings I banded over the years ate only white millet (from my feeders—they happily billed the weed seed in my scrubby fields). In my New England yard, no one likes white millet. You experiment and advance in knowledge by degrees. Isn't that what all of life is for?

A broad tray, raised off the ground out of reach of animals, if necessary with a squirrel baffle on its pole, is invaluable. Set on it kitchen scraps, white-bread crumbs (for some reason, birds don't like dark bread), cereal, pie crust, potato chips, fruits, meat scraps and bones, fish (catbirds are fond of fish), sweet potatoes, popcorn, stale peanuts. Ground eggshells supply needed calcium to nesting birds; cantaloupe, watermelon, squash seeds should be broken to make the kernels available. (I told you feeding was work—whether for birds or birders.) Dog food, cat food. In winter, when the ground is frozen or snow- or ice-covered, grit is important—sand, dirt, ashes, charcoal, small pebbles, again ground eggshells. A feeder needs some sort of shelter from rain or snow and should be cleaned regularly to prevent mold. Do you like moldy food? It was your idea to start feeding birds. If you are going to do it, do it right.

Suet: I keep a container of beef (or lamb, if beef is out of supply) suet hanging from an exposed branch too slight to support a raccoon or possum. I put suet in it every day—well, nearly every day—12 months a year. In summer, breeding birds are always at it, obtaining extra energy. They bring their chicks, teach them how to handle this bonus behind bars. Woodpeckers, titmice, orioles, catbirds, chickadees, jays, some warblers come to it, are dismayed if it is empty. My suet doesn't get rancid—it doesn't have time to. To be safe, I don't put out much at a time in hot weather, but I keep some there. The yellow-rumped warblers that eke out winter in my bay-berries understand the suet feeder but dislike it; they wait for jays and woodpeckers to knock crumbs on the ground. If no friendly suppliers come along, they fly up, peck some out to fall, then drop down and eat it. Catbirds in summer do the same.

In bookshops, nature-center shops, from Audubon societies, instructions in the many books written on bird-attracting give advice on mixing clarified suet or just bacon fat with corn meal, oats, nuts, raisins, peanut butter, crumbs, etc. I live in squirrel country, where containers of these would be promptly eaten. And, besides, I find this too much trouble—it is easier, less time-consuming, just to put out suet and seeds. In spring, I spike half oranges on branches, wiring these down so crows don't make off with them. Migrants, nesting orioles and cat-birds, an occasional warbler come to them. Sally Spofford in Arizona has listed some 23 species that come for the sugar water she puts out for hummingbirds. She uses small kitchen jars as well as commercial feeders. Red squirrels come to mine, chipmunks and nocturnal animals, though these latter aren't any fun since you can't see them thieving. Red coloring is helpful in attracting hummers at first, but once they have dis-covered a steady source of supply, they will come without it. A spoonful of honey initially gives a fragrance that attracts them, but this should not be continued since honey promotes bacteria. In the Quebec woods, where flowers were scarce, I had hummingbirds buzz a red bandana hanging from my pocket.

Each year when we arrived, the hummingbirds recognized me as a sort of Harvest Goddess. They would fly right up to me, drink from the jar I hastily filled and held out to them in my hand. They have done this in other localities, too, and sipped from my husband's twilight highball glass, if his drink had sugar in it (much to his surprise!). The usual proportions are 1 sugar to 4 water.

What else do birds eat? The gaping mouths of chuck-will's-widows can swallow a small warbler. A herring-gull pellet picked up by a Massachusetts Audubon Society tern warden contained aluminum foil and plastic, newspaper, glass from a Coca-Cola bottle, and (who says gulls don't watch television?) a Rolaids wrapper.

Epilogue

I told you way back at the beginning of this book that I am not much of a cook. Where I want to be is out in the field with my binoculars and notebook, a peanut-butter sandwich in my pocket, an apple, wondering (if I think about food at all) what some generous person willing to stay at home is cooking for us.

As far as my own hospitality is concerned, I feel there is nothing easier, safer, and able to go further than a ham—a half or whole ham that has been slathered with mustard and brown sugar, stuck with cloves, basted with pineapple juice, ringed (if you wish to be that elaborate) with canned peaches and pineapple. Ham can be used hot, cold, reheated. It creates leftovers and black-bean soup—it's ideal. Accompany it with macaroni and cheese, with vegetable casseroles or salads (why do we bother with anything else?).

WEST INDIES APPLE CHUTNEY

Well, you might want to enhance your reputation and, as a side dish, provide a bowl of this chutney.

Since fresh apples in the West Indies are in short supply, the recipe from there calls for 1 20-ounce can of pie apples, drained and chopped, ½ cup each of dark raisins and honey, 3 tablespoons of cider vinegar, a dash each of salt and ginger, ¼ to ½ teaspoon each each of dry mustard and curry powder. Stir these together, and cook to the desired consistency.

That's enough about ham.

A friend seeing me off to the city once picked up my tote bag and inquired as to its lumpy contents. A ham bone, I told her, for my editor. I have an appointment with him. He likes it for soup. There's a loaf of bread in there, too, for him, a peanut-butter sandwich for me in case my plane is delayed, a book. I believe in preparing for emergencies. Often there isn't time to catch a snack at airports.

"And a small flask of rum, I see," she said, exploring. "That's for emergencies, too?"

I nodded. Traveling across the continent once in the days when this took eleven hours, my seat in the plane broke, I was moved to a chair in the lounge. The chair had a short back; no way I could stretch out and sleep away the miles. I propped my head wearily on my hand and did the best I could. Somewhere over Bryce Canyon a stewardess awakened me to ask if I would like a drink. She had no sherry, no rum. "Water," I requested. "Maybe a little orange juice with it?" The men who had joined me in the lounge while I slept looked at me commiseratingly, nursing stronger spirits in their hands. Then their eyes widened as I took my small traveling flask from my bag, poured enough rum into my orangeade to revivify me, fortify me for the small grandchildren soon to be clambering over me. They smiled. With this one simple gesture, I acquired new friends. One of them was an eminent scientist. I have since followed his career. I wonder if he has equally followed mine?

Go back a page, I became diverted.

ELEPHANT STEW

If ham is too ordinary, too plebeian, for your taste, you can fall back on this.

Cut 1 medium-sized elephant into bite-sized pieces. (This

should take about 2 months.) Add enough brown gravy to cover. Cook for about 4 weeks at 465°. Will serve about 3,800 people. If more people are expected, 2 rabbits may be added. But do this only if necessary.

Now you are on your own. Happy cooking.

Addendum

"Elephants take too long to cook. Besides, they are becoming an endangered species," said my new friend Margaret Collins. She was squatting on our Caribbean island terrace, whacking a green coconut with a machete to obtain her daily-before-breakfast drink of coconut milk.

"Termites are easier and abundant. They cook up in no time. Just drop them in a little hot oil. Cook them until they puff and look crispy, then drain and salt them lightly. Cooked they taste like shrimp, raw rather like pineapple—it depends on the kind. You must get them before they metamorphose, though, while they are still tender and the wings haven't developed. Don't bother with North American ones—they are far too small. You have to be in Central or South America. The best are in Guyana."

She pulled from its scabbard the hunting knife she always wore and dug into one of the shaggy brown, broken termite nests, the ones she must climb trees to obtain, that were scattered about our steps. "Some are so fat the natives use them for oil. I collected a jar full in our bathroom last night, coming for the light. You were sleeping soundly. I hope the light didn't bother you. I planned to cook them for our breakfast, but someone in the kitchen knocked over the jar; they got away."

She sheathed her knife, wiped off her machete. We repaired to the main terrace for a fine, conventional breakfast of orange juice, omelet, and Jones sausage. Bananaquits joined us, sipping at the sugar and marmalade bowls. Crested Antillean hummingbirds explored the flowers. I didn't really miss the mess of termites she had hoped to serve me.

Index

INDEX